Do you panic at the thought of investing your money? Do you run and hide when your husband tries to teach you how to balance the checkbook or record your family's expenses? Were you raised to believe that money management is "men's work"? As the head of your household, do you regret that you've never learned how to budget, clip coupons, or organize a garage sale?

If the answer to any—or all—of the above is "yes," then you've come to the right source. You're about to make a move toward financial awareness. In *From Money Mess to Money Management,* Patricia H. Rushford introduces you to personal finance and investing. She shares hundreds of money-making and money-saving suggestions. You'll learn how to handle credit wisely, shop for values, choose a financial counselor, open a savings account, and much more. At the same time, Pat Rushford includes biblical illustrations that emphasize the importance of being a good steward of your God-given resources. You'll discover that the methods presented here will make you financially aware and capable in a very short time. Why not begin your journey to financial freedom today?

Books by Patricia H. Rushford

Have You Hugged Your Teenager Today?
The Care and Feeding of Sick Kids
From Money Mess to Money Management

From MONEY MESS to MONEY MANAGEMENT

Patricia H. Rushford

Power Books

Fleming H. Revell Company
Old Tappan, New Jersey

Scripture quotations identified TLB are from The Living Bible, copyright © 1971 by Tyndale House Publishers, Wheaton, IL. Used by permission.

Scripture quotations identified NASB are from the New American Standard Bible, © The Lockman Foundation 1960, 1962, 1963, 1968, 1971, 1972, 1973, 1975, 1977.

Scripture quotations identified RSV are from the Revised Standard Version of the Bible, copyrighted 1946, 1952, © 1971 and 1973.

Library of Congress Cataloging in Publication Data

Rushford, Patricia H.
From Money Mess to Money Management

"Power books."
Bibliography: p.
1. Finance, Personal. 2. Women—Finance, Personal.
3. Christians—Finance, Personal. I. Title.
HG179.R82 1984 332.024′042 83-24531
ISBN 0-8007-5141-8 (pbk.)

Published by Fleming H. Revell Company

Printed in the United States of America

TO

Ron:

my husband, partner, financial advisor,
my lover, and my friend

Acknowledgments

My special thanks to:

Ardes Burnes for the seed and Fritz Ridenour for planting the idea in my brain and having confidence that I could grow it into a book.

Ruby MacDonald and Lauraine Snelling for their unrelenting and caring critique.

Karen Jahnke, Sally Kaufman, Margo Power, JoAnne Coughran, Susan Fletcher, Lois Williams, Penny Brunnell, Angie Ensley, Lois Bourinski, and Ann Larson for their expert advice on saving money.

Sharon Davenport, Ginger Kreofsky, Verna Rocha, Jeanene Curtis, and Fern Janssen for their record-keeping secrets and successful budgets.

Dan Benson, John McKuen, Ron Rushford, and Jean Escorn for their financial expertise and for helping me inch up a couple of notches on the Financial Genius Scale.

Contents

Introduction

Financial experts tell us that only one-third of Americans are doing okay in handling their money. One-third are barely surviving, just managing to stay solvent. And one-third are in deep financial trouble—complete failures at money management.

My own experience is that at least two-thirds of all folks have real trouble balancing earning, giving, spending, and saving their money.

Christian authors and publishers have responded to this obvious need for financial help with an abundance of books and seminars on biblical money management. Having read most of these books and having been involved in many seminars, I've wondered what else needed to be written on this subject.

From the moment I started Pat Rushford's book, I was hooked by her creative, fun language. Her descriptions of women's money battles, the tantalizing spending temptations of busy mothers, and the special financial pressures of working women, made it obvious that this author has lived in the household maze where women live.

Whether single, married, divorced, or widowed, or whether employed outside the home or busy as a full-time homemaker, women will find this book has sound advice and practical ideas.

I've often sensed that most of us who wrote and taught biblical financial principles were men, who really did leave a gap in the kinds of information needed by women. *From Money Mess to Money Management* fills that gap.

Lots of products are touted with the claim that they don't cost—they pay. Anyone reading this book will easily be able to save its cost by putting into practice, for one week, any one of several excellent ideas offered in each of the seventeen chapters.

Although this book was written for women, I enjoyed it thoroughly. It is the kind of light reading that could help most men understand the different financial roles of their wives and daughters.

We've all heard that most of us don't use our God-given creativity very well. Every chapter of this book stimulated my creativity. If it does that for every reader, and in the process makes the stewardship of your money and possessions more pleasing to God, then Pat Rushford will have succeeded in her purpose.

George Fooshee

1

Financial Geniuses and the Rest of Us

"I'M AWARE OF MONEY—*ACUTELY* AWARE OF MONEY. IN FACT, I can't do without money. It just doesn't stay with me long enough to build any sort of lasting relationship." My friend Tilly echoes the thoughts of many women I've interviewed about financial awareness and money management.

Nearly every woman I meet expresses her desire to understand more about money matters.

"If you want to know more about money," I asked my friend Tilly, "why don't you read a book on it? The library is full of them."

"I know," sighed Tilly. "Don't think I didn't try. I picked up one of those 'money books.' It had more pages than the New York telephone directory. It was almost as easy to understand as the unabridged version of *Moby Dick.* By the time I plowed through the first chapter, I felt more confused and frustrated than a shepherd at a cattleman's convention."

"You must have learned something," I said.

"Sure," Tilly teased. "I learned that if I were to rate myself from one to ten on the Financial Genius Scale, I'd weigh in at a minus three."

Financial Genius Weigh-In

Of course, Tilly was exaggerating. If I were to score her I'd give her at least a one.

Where would you rate on the Financial Genius Scale? I have a feeling, since you picked up this book, you'd select a spot toward the middle range. However, depending on your day, you may classify yourself near the bottom—or dangerously close to the edge.

I am a six. I used to be a three, but since I began my research and wrote this book I added another three points. As you may have guessed, *From Money Mess to Money Management* is dedicated to the financially "insecure" woman, and the money "mismanagers," who rate anywhere from seven to zero and below. It's written for women who care about money matters and simply need a book that offers money facts in an easy-to-read-and-understand style. In fact, it was Tilly who inspired my most basic bookkeeping method—the one I call, Toss-it-in-a-drawer-till-tax-time.

I have great empathy for women who gravitate toward the lower end of the Financial Genius Scale. Perhaps it's because I feel intimidated by "tens" like Fran. Fran wrote the book, *How to Be Financially Secure in Just 2,769 Easy Lessons.* Even the title catapults me to the bottom of the scale.

Not that Fran isn't a warm, sensitive, and loving woman. She is. It's just that where finances are concerned, we don't speak the same language. At times I even wonder if we're from the same planet.

Fran can't help it that she loves to work with figures. It isn't her fault that she lives for daybreak and the morning delivery of the *Wall Street Journal.* In money matters she is a genius. Fran has the Merrill Lynch bull eating daisies. When Fran talks, E. F. Hutton listens. She can't be bothered by nightmares over unbalanced checkbooks because it's not on her list of things to do.

At fourteen, when most kids are investing in antiacne gels and designer jeans for their "bods," Fran bopped into money markets and real estate. She paid off her orthodontist with money she'd collected from rental properties and "hot tips" on the stock market.

Tilly, on the other hand, would love to move up the Financial Genius Scale, but . . . Well, turning a Toss-it-in-a-drawer-till-tax-time Tilly into a Financial Fran is . . . is . . . Let me put it this way: Would you ask a leopard to lay eggs?

When E. F. Hutton talks to Tilly, she has to hire an interpreter. To her, a *bull market* is when Merrill Lynch crashes through the walls of the stock exchange.

Taxes make Tilly about as agreeable as a cat in a dog pound. "I can't help it," she pouts. "It takes me over a year to recover from the tax-time trauma. Maybe if the year had thirty-six months instead of twelve I could adjust."

And budgets? Tilly tries, it's just that she usually runs out of money before she runs out of month. It's best not to talk with Tilly about budgets—at least not for a while. All I did was ask her if she'd make me up a sample budget for the book and she ranted.

"Budget? Ha!" Her laugh bordered on hysteria. "The baby has been crying for the last three hours with colic. While I rocked her, Kevin—he's two you know—poured a bottle of Joy in the dishwasher and turned it on. I'm having enough trouble keeping my mind in balance, let alone try for a budget. Oh . . . not again!" Tilly groaned. "Listen, I gotta go. Kevin just plugged the hair dryer into our beagle's nose."

Do you ever have days like that—or months? While you may not be in danger of falling off the Financial Genius Scale, like most women, you probably could use some help.

With all our responsibilities, like children, husbands, housework, and part- or full-time jobs, who has time to think about money management?

The majority of women I've interviewed say, "I'd like to learn about money management and investing, but I don't have the time." A surprisingly large number of women had no intention of getting involved in financial affairs.

One of those women, Victoria, winked and said, "Manage money? Me? No thanks! I'll leave that mess to my husband. Besides," she grinned, "making money and running the family finances is his job. Mine is to spend it."

Manage Money? Me?

While spending the money their husbands earn and enjoying financial freedom without the restrictions and responsibilities of money management may seem like great sport, these women are not being realistic. After all, what happens when their "protector" is no longer on the scene.

That won't happen? Let's hope not, but before you cancel yourself out of a financial education, look at these facts.

1. Women live longer than men. Nearly all my professional resources on money tell me I will probably outlive my husband. Consequently, I must be prepared to step into the role of breadwinner.

2. According to the 1983 Almanac, divorce occurred at a rate of one for every two marriages in 1981. Perhaps you are saying, "I don't believe in divorce," or, "It will never happen to us." Unfortunately, divorce can and does happen—often to women who least expect it.

3. The total percentage of American women who work has escalated from 43 percent in 1970 to over 50 percent today. According to the 1980 Census, it is estimated that almost two-thirds of the female population will be part of the labor force by 1990. This third fact shows that partly because of widowhood or divorce, women have been compelled to find part- or full-time jobs simply to survive.

Venita VanCaspel, in her book *The Power of Money Dynamics*, admonishes women who shirk their financial responsibilities. "If you are a woman," Venita warns, "don't ever think it is your inalienable right that a man should take care of your financial security. The single state—whether through choice, circumstances, death or divorce—will probably be your lot for at least a part or all your life. Even if you marry, you have an obligation to be a financial partner to your husband and to be as well informed as you can about money." Later, Venita adds, "In the past, too many women have been taught 'It's not nice to talk about money.' You'd better believe it's nice to talk about money—or you won't have any."

Just in case you're not convinced that you should be taking an active part in money matters, let me tell you about Ellen.

When forty-two-year-old Barney left home, forty-year-old Ellen couldn't believe it. She'd never expected divorce to soil their "blissful" marriage. But it did. Barney left Ellen lonely and tragically broke. She had no apparent means of securing a job or money. Ellen confessed, "I never paid much attention to our financial dealings. All I ever did was spend the allowance Barney gave me. I couldn't even balance a checkbook.

Ellen became what is commonly referred to as a displaced homemaker—unemployable, untrained, and in desperate need of money to care for herself and three children. In the divorce settlement Ellen was awarded their large Cape Cod home. "What good is a house," Ellen sighed, "when I can't afford the upkeep and the mortgage."

Ellen's story doesn't end there. Through a county assistance program and welfare services, Ellen received monthly allowances and the opportunity to attend a community college to learn a skill. She also learned basic record-keeping and budgeting skills. Today, Ellen manages her own business.

"If only I hadn't been so stupid," Ellen chided. "Every woman should have the good sense to at least know the basics in money management."

It is truly a wise woman who has learned and shared in the family financial responsibilities with her husband. Sharing the load not only brings you together as a team, it prepares you for the future. Even if you *know* you will never divorce, there is very little chance of your spouse living forever—at least not here on earth.

The time to learn is now. For Sarah, widowed at sixty-eight, time ran out. When George, her husband, died, he left a will and a substantial estate. Sarah should have been provided for, right? Wrong. Tragically, George never told Sarah where he kept his papers, his safe-deposit box, and other valuables. Without these documents, Sarah had no way of claiming her inheritance. In fact, she had no idea what her inheritance was. This couple made two terrible mistakes: George did not keep accurate records, and Sarah ignored their financial affairs.

Could these painful circumstances happen to you?

A Checklist for Financial Awareness

Here is a checklist to determine whether or not you need more financial understanding.

	Yes	No
1. Do you know what kinds of insurance you own and how it pays?	☐	☐
2. Could you locate those insurance policies now?	☐	☐
3. Do you know who to contact in order to collect the insurance premiums?	☐	☐
4. Do you know where and how your money is invested?	☐	☐
5. Do you and your husband have a will?	☐	☐
6. Do you know what the will contains?	☐	☐

	Yes	No
7. Do you know where the will is kept?	☐	☐
8. Has your husband taught you his record-keeping and filing system and told you what legal steps to take after he dies?	☐	☐
9. Are you aware of all sources of family income, including stocks, bonds, real estate, or other investments?	☐	☐
10. Do you know your current net worth, assets, and liabilities? Could you find out today?	☐	☐
11. Do you understand what records are needed for the IRS (Internal Revenue Service) and know where to find those records?	☐	☐
12. Do you now operate within a budget?	☐	☐

If you were able to answer yes to all of these questions, congratulations. I officially dub you, a Financially Aware Woman. Perhaps you missed on a point or two, or twelve. It's not too late to learn. Personally, I can't be content to let my husband "take care of me." I think it's unwise to remain ignorant of financial affairs that directly affect us and our families.

How Financial Can You Get

Maybe you are wondering, as I did, just how financially aware a woman should be. I remembered reading about the well-rounded woman in the Bible. Way back in 400 B.C. she is described in the Book of Proverbs.

> . . . she is worth more than precious gems! Her husband can trust her, and she will richly satisfy his needs. She will not hinder him, but help him all her life. She finds wool and flax and busily spins it. She buys imported foods, brought by ship

> from distant ports. She gets up before dawn to prepare breakfast for her household, and plans the day's work for her servant girls. She goes out to inspect a field, and buys it; with her own hands she plants a vineyard. She is energetic, a hard worker, and watches for bargains. She works far into the night! She sews for the poor, and generously gives to the needy. She has no fear of winter for her household, for she has made warm clothes for all of them. She also upholsters with finest tapestry; her own clothing is beautifully made—a purple gown of pure linen. . . . She makes belted linen garments to sell to the merchants. She is a woman of strength and dignity, and has no fear of old age. When she speaks, her words are wise. . . .
>
> Proverbs 31:10–22, 24–26 TLB

Wow! This lady was no slouch. Her financial endeavors were unlimited. She managed a household, invested in real estate, owned a vineyard, hunted for bargains, operated a garment industry, and on the whole seemed financially secure. She was either prepared for retirement or had no intention of retiring. The lady was financially independent.

Most women would find it difficult to wear her tunic. But, since I find the description in the Bible, I can't discount it. Anyway, I brought it up not to make you feel guilty, but to show that women can and should take an active part in the money game.

Come on, be honest with me. Didn't you like the part about planning work for the servant girls? I could live like that. While I can't promise you wealth and financial independence as you read this book, I *can* give you better understanding, and laughter in the learning.

Neither can I promise that by reading this book you'll turn into a "ten" like Fran; that is unless you want to and have a bent toward financial agility. You may never be a ten on the Financial Genius Scale, and that's okay, because Fran, dear as she is, totters on the bottom end of the scale in artistic abilities and pulls a seven in homemaking skills. (And you were beginning to think she was perfect.)

We all have different skills and abilities. And, although my book may not transform you, it can give you financial help no matter where you tip the scale.

Saunter through these pages and find out how you can catch up with the runaway money-eaters. Learn how to save money on almost everything you buy. Discover the money-makers and how you can take control.

After the money-eaters, money-savers, and money-makers, we'll hit the nitty-gritty of budgeting and record keeping. Did I hear a groan? Actually, it's not as bad as it sounds. Ask Tilly. Even she can adapt to my Toss-it . . . bookkeeping style. Instead of setting impossible goals of detailed records, you'll find a gradual incline. You can choose the simplest system, or most complex, or settle anywhere in between.

Remember, this is a money book designed with you, the busy, active woman, in mind. The transition from caterpillar to butterfly isn't made in a day. The transformation from Toss-it Tilly to a . . . well, to whatever level you have in mind, will take time. So relax. Enjoy. Let yourself grow.

PART I
The Money-Eaters

"Money disappears out of my pockets faster than fleas off a drenched dog."

"My budget is so full of holes, you'd think it had been hanging in a moth-infested closet."

Is your money more illusive than your kids on cleaning day? If so, stay tuned. This section, aptly named "The Money-Eaters," will show you where your hard-earned money disappears.

We'll uncover the nibblers like Miscellaneous, and gulpers such as Charge and Credit, and Minimarts.

Through the revelation of where the money goes, you'll also gain a clear picture of how you can put those money-eaters on a starvation diet.

2 Miscellaneous-Nibblers

HOW MUCH OF YOUR MONEY MYSTERIOUSLY ENDS UP IN your "miscellaneous expense" column? Do your total miscellaneous expenses surpass the national debt? When I first set up a budget and had to account for all my expenditures, my "misc" column had more figures than the European Health Spa. More money had been nibbled away by miscellaneous than by any other category.

Where Did All the Money Go

In order to manage money with any degree of accuracy, we should be able to account for at least 80 percent of those frittered finances. At first I blamed the money disappearance on my husband. "You're buying too many cups of coffee and newspapers," I cautioned. "And how many Cokes and donuts do you devour every day?"

After a quick calculation, Ron came up with, "My morning coffee comes to about $8, newspapers about $7, Coke runs the same as coffee, and I only have three or four donuts a month. That only comes to $24 a month."

"Well," I sighed, "that accounts for 10 percent, only 70 percent to go." As I tracked back through the last month's expenses, I tried to remember where all the entries labeled "cash" had gone.

Day one: Student loans, $2.00 (my kids hit me up for extra cash); Dr. Pepper, $1.50 (I have this addiction . . .); a Sugar Daddy, 30¢ (I needed a sugar fix); bus fare, 35¢; and a bagel with cream cheese from the vending machine at work, 65¢ (the hungries). Hmmm, $4.80 in one day . . . (gasp) that's nearly $150.00 a month.

Day two: Dr. Pepper, 50¢ (I've got to quit drinking this stuff. Oh well, I don't drink coffee . . .); Sego, 99¢ (I was on the run—and a diet); gas and oil . . . and . . . I couldn't go on. My memory went blank. Buyer's amnesia, I think they call it.

All I could recall was a blur of Minit Marts, milk trips, kids' hands, books, batteries, bus fares, an occasional lunch with the girls, Chicken McNuggets, Burrito Supremes, Whoppers, pizzas, and Dr. Peppers.

There's no sense dwelling on the past, I decided. The only way to cope with those miscellaneous-nibblers was to start today. I would develop a diet plan to dwindle those budget destroyers down to size.

A Ten-Point Nibbler-Reducing Plan

I realized that before I could change the nibbling habits, I would have to find out what they were. Thus, my first plan of attack was to keep track of my expenses. Through a series of trial experiments, I finally found a way to bring the nibbling miscellaneous column under control. Follow these steps to curb your nibbler's appetite.

1. *Keep a Record.* For one week, keep a note pad in your wallet or handbag. Write down and account for every penny. Sound like work? You bet. The purpose is not to create more paperwork for you, but to help you see how your money disappears. This recording process makes us aware of how much we spend and what we spend it on.

2. *Develop Awareness.* As you record expenses, your awareness level sharpens. Once I became aware of certain habits, and because of my aversion to detailed record keeping, I spent less. For example, if I stopped at a minimart for a soft drink and knew I'd have to take time to record the expenditure, I'd mutter, "Forget it." I became more and more alert to my habitual stops at stores and fast-food chains. I also realized how much gas money came out of my cash supply. And speaking of gas, do you know how much it really costs to run an automobile? Cars don't just nibble, they *devour.* For an honest and shocking account of what it costs to own and run an auto, read *You Can Beat the Money Squeeze,* by George and Marjean Fooshee.

3. *Keep It Going.* While one week of tight record keeping will help you determine where your money has been going, you'll want to take precautions against falling back into your old habits. Since it takes a month to develop a habit, it takes at least that long to break an old one. Make a pact to continue the records for one more week; then one more; and one more.

There you have it—a month. By that time, your awareness check system and recording will have become routine.

At each week's end, record those miscellaneous expenses under the appropriate headings in your expense file or ledger. Anytime you eat out, even when it's at the "Golden Arches," the expense should be included under *Food.* If you pick up a belt at a local boutique, the amount you spend should come under *Clothing.* By the time you've finished that nibbler called Misc will be slimmer than a gnat's elbow.

4. *One at a Time.* Each week of your miscellaneous-reduction diet, eliminate one more money-eating habit. For instance, are you into minimarts? Pass them by for one whole week. How did it feel? Did you miss them? Remember, these quick-stop shops didn't used to be available, and we survived without them.

Keep your quick-stop abstinence up while you cancel fast foods during week two. Soon, you'll have the worst money-eaters deleted from your spending menu. Read more about the ravenous food mongers in chapter 4.

5. *Wait Until Tomorrow.* "Never put off until tomorrow what you can do today." Good advice—for every area of life except spending money. In order to delete expenses and reduce money output, I've changed the saying to suit our monetary needs: "Put off until tomorrow what you can buy today."

6. *Fritter Money.* Once your miscellaneous expenses have slimmed down to the little odds and ends that belong there, you can ease off on the recording. If figures still hover above 1.5 percent of your income, it may still be too high.

Give yourself a weekly miscellaneous allowance. Unless you fall back into your old habits and run out of money before you run out of week, don't worry about keeping track. It's okay to give yourself a small amount of money to fritter.

When I'm on a food diet, I set aside a few calories for fun. I can use these saved calories for anything I want—like chocolate mousse or strawberry cheesecake. If I don't get an occasional sweet, I get sour and discouraged.

Just so, the reward of extra spending money that doesn't need to be accounted for boosts my morale.

Otherwise, it's easy to get fed up with reducing and blow the budget we're working so hard to restore.

7. ***Take Only What You Need.*** Carry only the cash you need. When I go to work, I take only enough cash to get me through the day. If I eat before work and take my lunch from home, my money needs are zero. An empty pocketbook, for those days when I'm surrounded by goody-filled vending machines, can save me and my budget's diet. (No credit cards or checks please.)

8. ***Reward Yourself.*** Say through diet discipline you manage to save ten dollars during week one, or even one dollar, or ten cents. Put that savings into a special account and watch it grow. Within a year you may have enough to pay for a trip to Florida, Mazatlán, or Hawaii. Or, it may just cover an emergency dental bill.

"A dental bill! That's no reward," you may be storming.

Actually, having saved enough money to pay cash for a dental bill is probably a greater reward than a vacation. Think how exhilarated you'll feel being out from under that oversized debt.

9. ***Spend It Better.*** The other day I stood behind a couple in a Minit Mart. I couldn't believe my ears. They asked the clerk for seventy-five dollars' worth of lottery tickets. I bit my lip.

"You fools," I wanted to scream, "how could you throw away money like that? There are millions of people starving in the world. Seventy-five dollars could feed a family of four for a week or two."

I was outraged. As I scooted into my car, I glanced at my purchases: a bottle of Dr. Pepper and a candy bar. I swallowed hard. That would have bought a half-gallon of milk or a pound of hamburger. I stood convicted. If I were going to judge my neighbor for spending seventy-five dollars on a chance, I had to judge myself for buying junk. Although the amount I blew was less, the sin remained the same. Maybe my fritter fund should go to feed the hungry.

10. ***Daily Discipline.*** The Lord teaches that we are to be disciplined disciples. While it usually doesn't work to try a complete transformation of your way of life in one day, all of us can change "little by little, one step at a time."

"For the moment all discipline seems painful rather than pleasant; later it yields the peaceful fruit of righteousness to those who have been trained by it" (Hebrews 12:11 RSV).

Reducing your miscellaneous-nibblers probably isn't going to be an easy task. It certainly hasn't been for me. It takes determination and discipline—and time. Don't try to rush through and change all these money-eating habits all at once.

I caution you in this because I wouldn't want you to be overwhelmed as you delve into the next two chapters where you'll meet more money-eaters, alias Big Gulp, and the Fast-Food Gang. So read on and enjoy. Then, put your money-eaters on that much needed diet.

3

Credit-The "Big Gulp"

While the miscellaneous-nibblers threaten to nibble you out of hundreds of dollars worth of loose change, the credit-gulpers could easily gulp down enough money to drain your life savings and eat you into bankruptcy.

Charge!!

This particular chapter has been devoted to the one word that has come to mean more to the American public than *Mom* or *Apple Pie. CHARGE!* We face more avenues through which we can "buy now and pay later" than there are freeways in Los Angeles.

After all, buying on credit can get us what we want now without the age-old hassle of being able to afford it. Advertisers tell us we can stroll down easy street as long as we carry "the card."

I know, I know, you're probably saying to yourself, *she's going to tell me to cut up all my credit cards and live on a cash-only basis.*

No, I'm not. I will ask you to check your spending habits like you did with the miscellaneous-nibblers, but I won't tell you credit is the forbidden fruit of our culture.

Positive and Negative Credit

In fact, there exists a certain type of credit buying that can be beneficial for our financial growth and development. I refer to this type of credit as *positive credit.*

Positive credit can help our financial situation and build our securities. Positive credit includes loans for a home or other real estate, or a business venture. Borrowing money for investments like these, if done with wisdom and understanding and prayer, may in time, increase your net worth because they will most likely increase in value.

Of course, if there is positive credit, there must be *negative credit.* And, boy, is there ever! In opposition, negative credit stands for all those credit cards and installment loans that decrease in value. Cars, appliances, stereos, clothing, and so on lose value—practically overnight. Overuse of negative credit can be hazardous, if not devastating, to your financial security.

With credit on the increase and practically every family playing the game, you probably never considered that you might not be eligible for it.

A Credit Rating of Your Very Own

Personally, I had never given credit much thought. I always figured if I needed credit, it would be mine.

"Not so!" declared Charlie.

Charlie Adams is my friend and financial genius. While other women would gaze at my achievements and wonder, *How does she do it?* Charlie, although she never said it, thought of me as a coward. She never forgave me for abandoning her on the ERA platform. "You could be great," she shouted.

"My family needs me," I reasoned. Sometimes I wonder what would have happened if I'd stood by her side. She made her fortune in the feminist movement selling "I Am Woman" pins. But, despite the fact that we didn't always agree on the rights of women, we've remained friends. In fact, when she heard about the money book, she invited me out to lunch.

"A housewife's money book," she smirked. "Darling, no one is married to a house. It won't sell you know."

"Charlie," I defended, "there are a few of us who don't mind the title. In fact I hear there's a new movement out to get women back home if they don't really want to work out."

After a sharp intake of breath Charlie exclaimed, "Where did you hear that?"

"I've read articles. One woman wrote a confession called "Freedom from Liberation." She admitted that work outside the home had never appealed to her. She blames the feminist movement for sweeping her along with the tide to an office job in the Bronx. When her husband opposed, her peers convinced her he was a chauvinist and had no right to interfere in her life. The woman related that she nearly lost her family to divorce. For two years she shoved her way through mountains of paperwork during the day and laundry and dishes at night. Finally she asked herself what she really wanted out of life. Home! She quit. The load of guilt fell from her shoulders like a robe of nails. Freedom. Freedom to be a den mother, to bake cookies. Yes—*homemade cookies.* She didn't care if the other women laughed at her and called her a housewife. It was what she wanted. I tell you Charlie it was a heart-wrenching story."

"It's a wrenching story all right. It makes me want to throw up."

"Oh, Charlie," I soothed. "Let's put our differences behind us. I need help on my money book."

Charlie, being the financial whiz she is, found a missing element right away. "You didn't include the importance of establishing credit."

"Huh," my eyes held a blank expression, and I knew I'd indiscreetly shown my ignorance.

"Don't you know? Every woman, married or single, *must* establish her own credit rating!"

"Why?" I asked.

Charlie, in a patronizing tone explained. "If your husband left for some reason and all your credit ratings were in his name, where would you be?"

"Home—and lonely," I mused.

"No, no," Charlie admonished. "You'd be back at the beginning. Without a credit rating you probably couldn't buy a car, a house, or even get the heat turned on."

"But I already have all those things," I retorted.

"Oh, my dear, how naive you are. Look. In my business I see women every day who suddenly find themselves separated, divorced, or widowed. I hear the same story over and over. Unless they had established credit in their own names, many women found themselves ineligible for credit cards or loans. Take Rose, for example. Rose told me she felt like she'd spent the last forty-five years in a vacuum. She'd always had credit. Now that her husband Bill had died, she couldn't even get a telephone. 'It was like I never existed,' she said. Can you imagine her humiliation when she had to ask her son to cosign for a phone hookup?"

"It doesn't seem possible," I frowned. "Didn't Bill leave her anything?"

"That's the sad part. He was a millionaire. Unfortunately, when his heart stopped, so did his estate. Everything got tied up in probate. Rose nearly starved. She said, 'It was like sitting in a diamond mine with my hands tied.' Believe me. It happens. You may not need that credit rating right now, but if you don't get one, you'll be sorry later."

I Was a Stranger to the TRW Credit Data Computer

I thanked Charlie for her input and hurried home to get her ideas on paper. Her words hung over me like a set of drapes. After dinner that night I asked my husband's opinion.

"Honey, should a married woman worry about establishing her own credit?"

"Why do you ask?" His deep voice held just a note of suspicion.

I told him about my conversation with Charlie. "I just wondered if I should," I added. "—I mean . . . in case something happened to you."

Ron shrugged. "You can if you want. But, we have a will and everything is left to you. There's no need to worry about probate."

"I know. It's . . . I wonder if I could even *get* credit. Would you mind if I tried?"

"Go ahead. You won't have any trouble."

With Ron's okay, I plunged in and applied for a loan. He was right. With my job as a nurse—secure income—and my assets—half of what we owned and owed was mine—the bank considered me a secure credit risk. Because I couldn't let Charlie's warning go unheeded, I set about establishing a credit rating in my own name.

Charlie was right about one thing. As a married woman I had ceased to exist on the TRW Credit Data computer. What a shock. Suppose in the future one of my great grandchildren checked through microchip after microchip trying to find evidence of my existence. Would they confront their grandparents (my kids) with accusations that they never really had a mother? The nightmarish thought prodded me on.

Whether you would like a credit rating to prove your existence to future generations or simply because you would feel more secure about your financial future, here are some ways to get it—without going into debt.

How to Get a Good Credit Rating Without Feeding the Gulper

First of all, in case you're asking, "Okay, maybe I should have a credit rating, but what is it?" I'll tell you. A credit rating is a record of your past spending habits and paying performance. Creditors use it to check on whether or not you can meet your obligations. Proof of your ability to pay enhances your chances for a loan.

At this point you may want to check to see whether you're already on record. Perhaps you had established credit before you married. If so, have them change your name or add your married name to your maiden name. This credit check on yourself will probably cost you about five dollars, and can be accomplished by calling a credit-rating agency. TRW Credit Data is one that has offices throughout the United States.

If you find you really *don't* exist, at least on the computer's readout, and feel the need to be somebody, take these steps.

1. Apply for credit at a department store in your name only. Use your name, Rose Ann Turner, not Mrs. John Turner. This type of credit is easiest to get. However, I feel I must caution you. If a credit card in your hands turns into a superpowered money-eater, move on to suggestions 3 and 4.

2. If you and your husband already have several credit cards, write to one or two of the creditors and ask them to issue a separate account in your name. This new credit card of your very own should be used sparingly. Make occasional small purchases and always pay off the bill at the end of each month to avoid interest charges.

3. The next time you need to purchase a larger item, such as a washer, dryer, television, or microwave, charge it on a ninety-day, same-as-cash loan. Many retail stores offer this service to customers. You can have three months to pay it off with no interest. Secure the loan in your name. Avoid debt. Save the money and make payments from savings.

4. Open your own checking or savings account. Some women I know have a separate checking account for household expenses. Talk with your husband about the pros and cons of such an arrangement. And, be careful the bank charges don't eat all your money. If you have your own account, the bank can serve as a handy reference for a loan officer. You can also ask to have your banking record appear on your credit rating.

While a credit rating may be important, it is not the only consideration in determining whether or not you are a good credit risk.

The creditor will want to know if you have a stable job. A writer with a paycheck coming in at sporadic intervals will have a harder time securing a loan than an RN of ten years with a regular monthly income. You must also be able to prove that your assets outweigh your liabilities. If your net worth works out to be −$1,100 chances are the loan officer will consider you unstable—I mean an unstable risk—and usher you to the door.

Once you have established your own credit rating and gotten a few credit cards be careful you don't abuse the privilege and find yourself in debt with a poor rating. Remember why you've gone to all this trouble. You did it to avoid a future crisis. Right?

To Charge or Not to Charge

Of course whether or not you decide to charge anything is entirely up to you. My friends, Susan and George never buy anything on credit. I shouldn't say never because they did purchase their home with a bank loan.

"To us," George advises, "using credit cards and installment loans is like walking through a crocodile-infested swamp. Sooner or later they'll gobble up your assets. It's a dangerous game and you stand to lose a lot more than your shirt."

"There's a certain freedom in paying cash for everything," Susan added. "If we need something we save for it. While we're saving, we comparison shop and look for specials. When we hand over the cash, that's it. We don't suffer headaches over the next couple of months worrying about whether or not we'll have enough money to make payments."

"Didn't you need established credit to buy your home?" I wondered.

"Not at all," replied George. "We had saved enough for a down payment, and the bank loaned us the rest with the house as collateral."

"I think," Susan said, "if people buy on credit they need to be extremely well disciplined to avoid overspending."

"It's not just the overspending that eats up the money," I added. "Did you ever take a close look at those interest rates?"

Interest Rates—Read the Small Print

While a read-between-the-lines philosophy may help you better understand a love letter from your sweetheart, it will give you nothing but blank spaces on a credit card or loan agreement. Carefully read each line.

As you read the small print, you will notice a monthly percentage rate of only 1.5 percent (this amount varies). "That's not much," you may be saying. But, that little interest compounds to 18 percent a year. Many of the charge cards run about 21 percent yearly interest. If you had a $600 balance revolving in a credit card account for a year it could cost you $126 in interest charges. I don't know about you but I could find a better use for my money.

Budget dieters like us should be wary of where our money

is spent. Balances left over on credit cards, especially if you use several, tend to carry away a plump sum by the year's end.

Consumer loans, that is, loans based on your credit rating and ability to pay, have been running an average of 15 percent a year. While this is a little cheaper than the credit card loans, if you consolidated the same $600 into a loan such as this, your interest at the end of the year would be $90. I could feed my teenage son for two or three days on that.

Anytime you agree to use a business's money through a loan, whether it's credit card purchases or direct loans, you will be given a contract. Read it carefully. If you have questions, ask. Double talk that makes you feel like your mind's been through a blender should be treated with suspicion. Never sign anything you don't fully understand.

Don't worry about turning down a company that's offered to give you a loan. Shop around for the best deal. You as a woman have the right to get credit anywhere, providing you are a good credit risk. If you're not, you shouldn't be borrowing the money anyway. Moneylenders abound in our country and most of them wouldn't dream of taking your firstborn child as part of the down payment. However, they are out to make money, and interest rates earn them a bundle.

Know the Rules Before You Play the Game

Every game has its own rules and language. In order to play the game you need to understand what it's all about. For instance, in Monopoly you need to understand that too many "Go directly to jail without passing Go and do not collect $200," can jeopardize your real estate business. And even if you like purple better than blue, Boardwalk brings you a higher return on your money than Baltic.

In the credit game there are also rules as well as a financial lingo that you will want to learn before you play. Here are some rules that may help.

1. Be aware of and ready to fulfill your responsibility in repaying the loan. Know when the payments are due and how much they will be. Also be aware that the creditor can tack on a late charge. Of course the loan company won't mind if you're a few days late, they'll just demand five dollars a day or more in late charges.

2. Know the legal lingo. While I can't take the space here to write you a dictionary of financial terms, I will throughout the book give you explanations as I use them. If before signing a contract you come across a term you don't understand, ask someone; or if you're embarrassed, excuse yourself to the ladies' room and look it up in your dictionary. Better yet, ask to take a copy of the contract home with you so you can study it at your leisure and perhaps ask a trusted and experienced friend.

One woman I know of nearly lost her home because she signed on the line without full understanding of the contract terms. The contract called for a balloon payment at the end of five years. She thought at the time it was a strange request, shrugged it off as a quirk, and forgot it.

Five years later she got a letter threatening to foreclose if she couldn't come up with the balloon payment of $40,000. The "balloon" payment was the whole balance she owed on the house. Although she managed to secure a bank loan, she could have saved herself much grief by knowing the rules first.

3. Realize that lending institutions don't loan you money out of the goodness of their hearts, but because they make money on interest rates and fees. Consequently you are doing them a favor by letting them loan you money. I'm not telling you this so you can gain a sense of superiority, only so you won't feel lowly and intimidated.

4. Anytime you use a credit card you are borrowing money. If you pay off the balance in full each month you pay no interest and in fact will be using that institution's money for free.

5. Credit expands your buying power when used within the guidelines of your budget. It can ease the discomfort of expending large amounts of cash by allowing you to pay over a period of time. However, when you use that power as the pot at the end of the rainbow—and if most of your transactions are made on credit—you're probably in big trouble.

6. The more money you have, the easier it is to get a loan. Does that make sense? It's like the old saying, "Them that has gets." How true. The easiest loans to obtain at the lowest interest rates are those which are fully secured. In other words, if you want to borrow $10,000 and you have $10,000 in a savings account, the bank will loan you the money. They usually charge about 1 percent more than what you would be receiving in interest on the saved money. The $10,000 in your savings account is frozen by the bank until you've paid off your loan. It is used as collateral. I know, you're thinking, *That doesn't make any sense either. Why would anyone need to borrow money they already have?* Don't ask me. I really couldn't tell you. I think it's one of those strange rules someone made up when the board of directors were out to lunch.

7. The game is over for you when you fail to meet your financial responsibilities.

8. The credit game is a dangerous one. If you're not careful it can plunge you into a case of the "credit-card crazies."

Surviving the Credit Card Crazies

In a world where plastic money is as good as cash, it's easy to get ourselves overextended. The line we walk between safety and disaster in credit card use is as fine as the one between sanity and mindlessness. In fact, the way we behave when spending money depends a lot on our mind control. How much control do you have? Have you developed a case of the "crazies"? Here's a quiz that will give you the answer.

	Yes	No
1. Do you have six or more credit cards?	☐	☐
2. Do you use three or more of those cards on a regular basis?	☐	☐
3. Do you worry about whether or not you'll be able to make your credit card payments at the end of each month?	☐	☐
4. Have you been operating in the red for two or more months in a row?	☐	☐
5. Do you feel a pang of guilt when you pull out a card to pay for an item?	☐	☐
6. Do you often charge, knowing you don't have funds in the bank to cover that amount?	☐	☐
7. Do you buy small items on credit that you wouldn't buy or couldn't buy if you had to use cash?	☐	☐
8. Do you often pay only the minimum required balance on your charge statement?	☐	☐
9. Do you receive notices of late payments?	☐	☐
10. Does more than 20 percent of your income go for paying of credit card or installment loans?	☐	☐
11. Do you buy on credit to lift yourself out of the "I ain't got no money" blues?	☐	☐
12. Do you ever charge as a revenge tactic against the husband who says no?	☐	☐

Positive answers to six or more means you've developed a full-blown case of the credit-card crazies. Three to five affirmatives means you're mildly afflicted. One to two yes answers means exposure to the disease, and in order to survive, I suggest you immunize against further attack. Here are some guidelines that can nurse you back to sanity and help you sidestep further complications.

1. Use cash or your checkbook whenever possible.

2. Reduce the number of credit cards you carry with you. If you can remain disciplined and immune and never charge more than you can pay off at the end of the month, go ahead and keep your favorite cards. If you are crazed, with an out-of-control budget, even one card can mean disaster. For complete protection against the crazies, leave the cards at home. In severe cases of the crazies the only cure is surgery. Cut those plastic money munchers into guitar picks for your budding musician, or slip the tiny plastic chips in the garbage.

3. Refrain from buying when depressed. Do you ever experience mood swings? I do. In fact, the days just before my period I usually feel about as low as an alto with a cold. I think, *Maybe if I buy a little something just for me . . . ?* At times like these, my sales resistance is low and advertisers can make me believe anything. I'd like to take my "so-worldly, so-welcome" MasterCard and fly off to the Riviera, or slip into a designer sack from Saks. Instead, I should be praying, "Lord, lead me not into the temptation to charge."

4. If shopping really does lift your spirits, do it; only don't spend any money. If you just gasped and said, "I can't," relax, I'll tell you how. Leave your credit cards and checkbook *and* cash at home. Try on all the clothes you want. Be extravagant, you can afford it. Whenever you find the perfect dress, hat, shoes, bag, fur coat, or whatever, ask the clerk to hold it for you for an hour or so. Have your fling. When it's over, go home. List all those must-have items, if you can remember them, and rationally consider each one. Is it something you need? Can your budget handle the expense? If you decide the item needs you as much as you need it, call the store and ask them to hold it for you until you can come back.

Try it. You'll be surprised at how fast the love affair between you and your perfect hat ends. Usually, in these love-at-first-sight encounters, absence makes the heart forget. My tried-and-true method can waylay buyer's remorse hangover and anxiety attacks, symptoms of the crazies.

5. Pay your entire bill each month. I have devised a method of doing this which is entirely pain-free. Even the usually agonizing procedure of writing a check to pay the bill quiets into a dull ache. I list each charge as I make it in my checkbook and subtract it from the balance. Beside each entry I indicate which card was used. For example MC means MasterCard and AMX stands for American Express. At the end of each month I mark each entry with a yellow marker. I then add them up and subtract them from my total cash supply so I can balance the check statement. The amount I have deducted for charges will cover my bills and there's no chance of my not having enough money to pay it all off. I find this method cuts down on credit card use because, if I don't have the money in my checking account I won't buy.

Another method that works for a friend of mine is this. Keep a small diary or notebook in your purse. In it write each of your charge cards by name and set a limit.

	American Express		MasterCard		Nordstrom's
Limit:	$100		$100		$40
		1/12	−25	1/13	−23
			$ 75		$17
				1/27	− 6
					$11

As indicated, each time a charge is made, enter the amount and date under the appropriate heading and subtract from the credit limit. When you've reached your limit, stop charging. Keeping track of your day-to-day charges makes you painfully aware of where your money goes.

6. Pay off your debts as soon as possible. If you have allowed your credit card bills to zoom out of control, see about getting a consumer loan (at less interest) to pay your smaller bills off. If you must take this step to get yourself out of debt, then by all means, stop using the credit cards. The credit-card crazies can be much like alcoholism. If you have the disease, you must give up the habit "cold turkey" or you'll fall back into the same trap.

Although the crazies won't destroy your body like alcohol or drugs, and you probably won't die from an overdose, your budget could. You stand the chance of facing bankruptcy. In either case, you lose.

7. If you feel overwhelmed by your debts and can't get yourself out of debt, seek professional help. Many cities offer programs with counseling services. Portland, for example, has a nonprofit organization called Consumer Credit Counseling of Oregon. Check your phone book for help.

8. Consider the following thoughts while you decide whether credit cards and installment loans are for you.

Proverbs 22:7, ". . . the borrower is the slave of the lender." (RSV)

1 John 2:15, "Do not love the world or the things in the world." (RSV)

Romans 13:8, "Owe no one anything, except to love one another. . . ." (RSV)

I'm not trying to convict you or convince you that credit is an evil influence. Used for the right purpose and with deliberate control, it can make us better stewards of the money God allows us. Used wrongly, credit can control us. I for one don't want to be controlled by a plastic card god.

There is an account in Matthew 25, where a master leaves money in the hands of his servants. Two are faithful and are given more. One blew it and was chastized severely. He ended up with nothing. Is God happy with the way I handle money? Can He trust me with what I have and more? I wonder.

Ahem . . . excuse me while I prepare for surgery. It looks as though my kids won't run short of guitar picks for a while.

I'm sure we would all like to be what God considers good

stewards, but most of us fall short of our goals at times. Perhaps some of those falling-down times come under the heading of our next group of money-eaters—fast foods, conveniences, and minimarts. Join me and we'll teach those ravenous appetites some healthful abstinence.

4

The Ravenous Appetites of the Fast-Food Gang

IF YOU THINK THE MISCELLANEOUS-NIBBLERS AND THE great credit gulp take a giant-size bite out of your money supply, wait till you inspect the fast-food gang.

JoAnne Coughran, formerly food editor for *Virtue* magazine and author of a new book for Tyndale House, *Victory at the Supermarket*, revealed some startling food facts. In my interview with JoAnne she told me, "The biggest money monger in the United States is the fast-food industry. We're talking 'mega bucks' here. Did you know that McDonald's, maker of the Big Mac, is the largest food producer in the world?"

Fast-Food Facts

"You're kidding!" Her statement surprised me. "What about Del Monte and General Foods?"

She shook her head. "Shocking isn't it? But it's easy to understand when you consider the fact that over half of the families in the United States eat more than 50 percent of their meals out. The average family eats out six times a week."

"Six meals, huh?" I pondered her statement. "I think you're right. We manage at least that many with all the pizza, hamburgers, fish and chips, and tacos we consume. Although we don't indulge, I understand they even serve quickie breakfasts."

"Right. It's that quickie philosophy that gets us into trouble. Why waste precious time cooking, when you can grab a meal in a minute and a half? And, most people feel they're getting a bargain."

"Well, aren't they?" I countered. "I mean, a hamburger only costs a little over a dollar, and french fries. . . . What are they? Fifty cents?"

"Compared to restaurant dining, yes," JoAnne continued, "but when you compare fast-food prices to the raw materials from the grocer you can see the difference. As an example, for the cost of one burger, you can buy one pound of hamburger and perhaps even add in all the trimmings to feed four people. A one-pound bag of frozen fries equals the cost of a side order of ready-mades, and raw potatoes. . . . Well, you can see what I mean."

"Hmmm, I sure can," I agreed.

As we talked on about the fast-food industry, it became increasingly clear that we, rich and poor alike, spend one-fourth to one-third of our food budgets on fast or junk foods. This parallels the amount we should be spending on meat and protein sources.

"But," you may be protesting, "we don't count our meals out on the food budget."

If you don't, you're not alone. JoAnne says, "Most families don't count fast foods as groceries. They include the expense under entertainment. That's a no-no. *All* restaurant foods should come under groceries."

She's right you know. Have you seen those money pies that

divide your income into percentages? Well, according to some money pie experts, 20 to 24 percent of your total income should be budgeted for food—all food.

Some of you may need to rebudget your food allowance. If you do, be careful not to cut it down to an unrealistic size. That would be almost as discouraging as trying to squeeze a size-sixteen dieter into a size ten the day she decides to diet.

Often people who cut their estimated budget too small don't buy groceries, but they do buy more fast foods. After all, a couple of bucks in the pocket won't buy much in the way of groceries, but it will get me a hamburger and a Coke.

That's the rationale for getting into trouble. Financial troubles can lead to depression, depression may make you feel like running away. Running away, perhaps to a movie or dinner out, in hopes it will make you feel better. But it doesn't. The excursion may drive you further into debt and depression. Thus begins the cycle that wheels so many Americans down the road to financial ruin.

Second in Line—Prepared Foods

"You mentioned the fast-food industry as the largest monger, what's next—the grocer?" I asked JoAnne as our interview continued.

"Actually, no," she replied. "A lot of people think of the grocer as the culprit who makes a mint on all that food stocking the shelves. When you come down to the bare facts, the grocer makes only 1 percent net profit."

"So, all the money between raw materials and labor to the grocer's shelves must be taken up in processing," I offered.

"Exactly. The second worst monger in the food industry is convenience or prepared food. Foods like biscuit and cake mixes, frozen dinners, pizza—anything that comes practically ready to eat, fits into the prepared-foods category."

"Ow," I winced. "I'm more guilty of overbuying in that department than fast foods. I buy frozen pizzas to appease my foraging teenagers. Sometimes I feel like a lion tamer. 'Back! Back!' I yell, as I throw them a pizza or bag of chips to keep them from devouring a week's groceries before I get them put away. My son would prefer steak, but pizzas are cheaper.

"I'm mostly into basic foods myself—when I can find the time. I love to cook meals from scratch. Unfortunately when I ask my family to cook basic. . . . Well, let me put it this way. I'd get a more positive reponse if I told them to clean our cat, ChuLing's, litter box. Honestly, JoAnne, I need prepared foods. They keep my family from starvation when I'm not around."

"I understand," JoAnne sympathized. "Prepared foods can be a great help for working moms. There is one thing though. Most women are of the opinion that prepared foods save time."

"And they don't?" I asked.

"Not always. Most convenience foods are a matter of habit and don't necessarily save time."

"That's true, now that I think about it. There are many convenience foods I avoid because I can make my own just as fast—and homemade always tastes better. Take spaghetti sauce, for example. I can whip up a thick, savory, meat sauce in the time it takes to cook the spaghetti. It tastes like it's stewed in a cooker all day. The comparison to a store-bought variety would be like comparing filet mignon to beef bones.

"You can find the same is true with pancakes and waffles, Hamburger Helper, and macaroni and cheese. I scramble up a terrific goulash, with meat and noodles in less time than it takes to prepare the 'prepared' food."

Before you buy convenience foods, consider both cost and time saved. If you can do it yourself for less money, in equal time, and get a better end product, why pad the pockets of the food makers. I know my bare-bones budget would thrive on the savings.

Here are some final thoughts to help you over the prepared-foods hump. Take these thoughts with you when you shop.

- Your best buys are unprocessed foods.
- Coupons on processed foods don't always guarantee a bargain.
- Make it a habit to compare raw materials to ready-made products, as you calculate your available time.
- Eat at home.
- Use the most basic ingredients possible.
- Keep plenty of staples on hand so you can prepare those "quickie meals" in your own kitchen.
- Even if you're tight on time, make time to shop at grocery stores.
- Avoid the frequent pit stops at your local minimart.

The Minimart Temptation

Minimarts are handy. We have five of them within a one-mile radius of our home. Within minutes I can zoom in and pick up a jug of milk, a bag of chips, and a six-pack of Pepsi. Milk, I needed, the other stuff looked good.

While these stores can be a blessing when you run out of milk, they can gnaw away at your unsuspecting food budget with the miscellaneous merchandise you gather on the way out of the store.

These stores are designed to tempt you. I can almost hear them calling: "Feast your eyes and fill your tummy. Let us handle all your money."

You think I exaggerate? Go ahead. Try walking in and out of the store without getting more than you went in for. You need milk? It's in the back. There, past the ice cream, and the pretzels, way back on the other side of those colorful cans of soda pop. You made it back? Great. Now let's see you maneuver yourself past the M&Ms, milk chocolate, and licorice sticks. Like magazines, newspapers? The headlines lure you with captions like, "Learn the real story behind the Prince's unmatched socks . . . ," or, "The true story behind George's long life. Does he really operate on batteries?"

Okay, suppose you tear your eyes away from the gossip racks, you still have to wait at the counter. More candy, Rice Krispy bars, and . . . and . . . a chocolate glazed donut with custard filling. . . . Oh, help . . . I can't. . . .

Well, I didn't make it. Did you? I've decided there are only four ways to resist temptation in minimarts: 1. Don't go. 2. Blindfold yourself and rent a Seeing Eye dog. 3. Borrow blinders from an understanding horse. 4. Take only enough money to buy what you need.

No one knows better than I how difficult it is to escape the voracious jaws of the money-eaters. But regardless of our financial situation it's important that we get this food business in the right perspective. Let's face it. Fast foods and junk foods, as well as many prepared foods, don't contain the quality nutritional values our bodies require.

I believe we need to take a critical look at our eating habits as well as our spending habits. While I won't elaborate on the subject of eating better for less, I will direct you to some fantastic resources. Doris Longacre has written two exceptional books on spending less and eating better—*Living More with Less* and the *More-with-Less Cookbook.* Other excellent resources are, of course, JoAnne Coughran's *Victory at the Supermarket,* and *Diet for a Small Planet* by Francis M. Lappe.

The appetites of the fast-food gang are indeed ravenous. We will all do well to listen to the wise words of Little Orphan Annie as she spins a scarey tale and warns, "The gobble-ins'll git'cha if you don't watch out."

While we try to steer clear of the gobble-ins, and pursue our goal of being God's good stewards, sometimes our money still doesn't stretch as far as we'd like. If your money loses its elasticity faster than your underwear, and your expenses are as hard to meet as Robert Redford, I can help.

In the next few chapters, you will find dozens of ways to help you restretch those dollars. With all those money-saving ideas and fun ways to make money, you'll be able to fatten up your emaciated budget and maybe even broaden your profit margin.

PART II
Money Saved Is Money Managed

Saving money and starving the money-eaters takes time and talent.

Perhaps you're saying, "That leaves me out, because I have about as much time as the equator has ice. And talent . . . ha!"

Don't be too hasty. As for time, I know you have as much as I do. We're all given twenty-four hours a day, remember? Talent? Well, talent is in the hands of the doer.

Remember Toss-it-in-a-drawer-till-tax-time Tilly? Tilly refused to involve herself in organized bookkeeping for two reasons. First, she didn't want to; and second, Tilly wouldn't try. Who knows what talents lay tickling the undersurface of Tilly's mind and fingertips.

In this section you'll find scores of money-saving ideas from the experts. Read stories about bargain hunters, super sales sleuths, coupon clippers and refunders extraordinaire, negotiators, barterers, and do-it-yourselfers.

Saving money and living within your means needn't be the eyebrow-tweezing experience you may have thought. On the contrary, some women actually enjoy it. I, for one, find saving money exhilarating. It's like the feeling I get when my teenager comes home a minute and a half before curfew. My coupon-clipping and refunding friend, Linda, shares my excitement.

"The thrill I feel when I save all those bucks on my groceries is like running out of gas on top a hill and seeing a gas station at the bottom."

You'll want to read through these various money-saving techniques and choose those that fit your personality and life-style. Also, be sure to pick those that give you the most joy, and of course, the most profit.

Maybe you're not sure where your talents lie. And, time won't hang around long enough for you to use it. Perhaps you've never really had to scrimp and save or stretch dollars up until now because you've had it all. But, with today's shaky economy and skyrocketing prices you've concluded, "I either save money or starve." Perhaps these handfuls of helpful hints will come to your rescue.

5
Bargain Hunters and Super Sales Sleuths

BARGAINS ABOUND, YOU JUST HAVE TO KNOW WHERE to look for them—and when. Now, I'm not talking about those ho-hum 10 to 30 percent-off sales you find in almost every retail store. I'm talking 40, 50, 60 percent off, and sometimes even more.

Tales From the Super Sleuths

Let me give you some examples. My friend and super sales sleuth, Sally, needed new drapes. A local department store quoted her these prices:

Drapes	$511
Sheers	206
Subtotal	$717
Tax	45
Total	$762

Being an expert shopper, Sally comparison shopped and found a better price at a discount drapery outlet. This was their quote:

Drapes	$300
Sheers	163
Subtotal	$463
Tax	29
Total	$492

Wow! That's a whole $270 savings—35.5 percent. But, Sally had only $300 to spend on those drapes. Before she began her shopping expedition she'd asked God to help her find some for that price or less. The discounted price was still $192 too much.

"I'll wait for the Lord," Sally smiled. "He never fails me."

A week later, Sally felt strongly motivated to return to the discount store. She browsed through the ready-made draperies and found nothing. Sally then negotiated for better terms with the store manager—and succeeded.

"Three hundred and fifty," he stated. "Bottom line."

Sally sighed and said, "I'll wait." She made her way back through the ready-mades. "Maybe I should look through these one more time," she declared.

Then she saw them—on top of the pile. Her drapes—perfect color and style.

"What a coincidence," the clerk told Sally, "I just put those out."

"That was no coincidence," grinned Sally.

Sally's final heaven-sent price:

Drapes	$149
Sheers	99
Subtotal	$248
Tax	9
Total	$257

Sally saved $505, 66 percent over the original quote. She proved beyond a reasonable doubt, it pays to shop around and of course, to accept a little help from a Friend.

As a cut-above-second-rate bargain hunter, I've bagged a few big ones myself. Let me tell you about this terrific place I found. It's called CY's House of Samples. They have a large, moderately well-dressed salesroom where you can find savings up to 40 percent. B-u-t . . . out back, there's this naked warehouse where you can save 50 percent and more. That's where I headed.

Of course, I had to forgo salesclerks hovering at my elbows, plush burgundy-turquoise carpets, and mink-lined dressing rooms, but so what. The sagging, chipped panel partitions and orange polyester curtains afforded all the privacy I needed to try on my treasures. I found a wool skirt in a deep cranberry, my favorite color, for only $7.88 and fully lined tweed slacks. . . . But wait, here's a list so you can see for yourself the comparative savings.

	Retail	**CY's price**
Zado sweater—silk/angora	$ 37.00	$10.88
Jantzen tweed culottes—lined wool	62.00	8.88
Jantzen tweed slacks—lined wool	64.00	16.88
Jantzen skirt—soft wool	58.00	7.88
Jantzen cowlneck—acrylic/wool	24.00	7.88
Esprit split skirt—corduroy	30.80	5.88
	$275.80	$58.28

As you can see, my savings on this shopping spree totaled $217.52. Wow! Nearly 79 percent. Not bad, huh? The proof is in the purchases.

Hunt for Quality

While we're in the clothing section of this bargain bonanza, I'd like to direct your attention to quality. Just because bargain hunters and super sales sleuths frequent the discount stores, thrift shops, and bargain basements doesn't mean we have to give up quality workmanship or style. In fact, discount shopping means I can have the brands I want—for less. Oh, I admit, sometimes I have to do without the label, but for a difference of 50 percent or more—who cares?

Maybe you're asking how you can tell which clothes are manufactured by whom without a label. I wondered that too. Then I found this most fantastic book called *Dress With Style* by Joanne Wallace. In it she discloses a secret about bargain hunting that could revolutionize our shopping techniques. Joanne tells us that on each of the clothing articles, even if the label has been removed, we can identify the designer.

She says, "the Federal Trade Commission has now assigned identification numbers to manufacturers, and by law these numbers must be on all designers' garments." These identifiers are called RN & WPL numbers. For example, Jantzen's ID number is RN37966, WPLO6979, while Ralph Lauren Originals stakes the claim on RN56158. And, here's the best part. You can find this treasury of ID numbers in the *RN & WPL Directory* at your local library. I'd suggest you borrow it and write down your favorites on a three-by-five card. Keep it in your wallet for emergencies. If you're anything like me, your body has a built-in radar system for tracking sales. You pick up the signal. You become Super Sales Sleuth, and move in for the kill.

For times like those, weapons such as the RN & WPL IDs are indispensable. In her book, Joanne offers many more techniques that can help you "dress with style." She shares ideas on how to choose the right clothes for you, how to find your best colors, and how to dress tastefully and economically.

How to Find Bargains on Everything

So much for clothes. Now it's on to the exciting part. Clothes aren't the only items we want to save money on.

There are appliances, you know, those things that stop running so your kids or husband can get you new ones for your birthday or Christmas? And you'll want to save on carpeting, furniture, dishes . . . and, well, you name it. A serious saver will never pay the full price for anything. Fortunately, you don't have to. And you don't have to work hard at finding the most well-stocked hunting grounds either.

Much of the footwork has been done for you. Iris Ellis has written a book called the *Save on Shopping Directory.* In it she tells you the name and address and phone number of over seven thousand stores, indexed by state, where you can buy anything from a diamond ring to a potato masher. Shoes, designer clothes, fabrics, food, luggage, housewares, and more are included. What's more, she updates the book on a regular basis.

Another source that tells you where to find whatever you are looking for is the *Underground Shopper.* I read an article in the magazine *Executive Female* about the author of this publication, Sue Goldstein. Sue is in the business of letting us—the consumers—know where to find the best buys. For information write to: *Underground Shopper,* SusAnn Publications, Inc., 3110 North Fitzhugh, Dallas, Texas 75204. (Phone 214-528-8970.)

Although these where-to-find-it books may be helpful, they won't be able to uncover all the secret places where bargains hide. Here are a few tips to help you locate the big game.

1. Check out the thrift stores, secondhand shops, Goodwill, and Salvation Army. You'll find them listed under "Thrift Shops" in your telephone directory. These can be an excellent source for children's clothes, toys, and sometimes adult clothes too. On my last visit to the Goodwill, I found a Levi's shirt for my teenage son for only $2—perfect condition. It takes a little more time to find true bargains in some of these stores; but when the hunt brings forth a bonus buy, it's worth every minute.

2. Look in the yellow pages under the item you want to buy. For example, "Women's Apparel—Retail" and "Women's Apparel—Whsle & Mfrs.", or "Appliances—Retail" and "Appliances—Whsle & Mfrs.", would be a good place to start. As you skim through the entries look for key words like *factory outlet, samples, manufacturer, discount, bargain, used,* and *secondhand.* I prefer the factory outlets and sample shops. Both offer new merchandise at used prices. Before you visit manufacturers, call. They may not sell retail.

3. Check out your local newspaper ads and classified section. Key words here are *garage sales, bankruptcy sales, estate sales, clearance sales, factory closeouts, liquidation,* and *auctions.* Beware of some of these "spectacular sales." Some companies go out of business every month. And a store's assets can be liquidated every day—it's a matter of selling the merchandise and getting cash in return. Be sure you know an item's worth before you shop. Merchants have been known to dupe the public into believing they're getting something for nothing, when in fact, they are really getting *nothing for something.* Be wary of big clearance or super sales where salesmen swarm around their customers like hawks around a chicken coop.

4. Pop into your local chamber of commerce. Some cities have enterprising groups that offer tours through their factory outlets and discount stores. I've recently heard of a service such as this in Seattle. The tour includes lunch and a bus ride to businesses that offer the best bargains in town. Of course there is a fee, but what a fun way to find a bargain. And maybe, if the idea excites you, you could start your own tour business. Just think, you'd make money as well as save money while you shop.

5. Don't forget your local retail stores. Early spring and early fall are two of the most likely times for super sales. This is when stores try to rid their inventories of seasonal items. Holiday sales, like Washington's Birthday, Fourth of July, Labor Day, seem to encourage drastic price reductions. The other day, Jantzen Beach Mall had a Presidents' Day sidewalk sale. I found a quilted leather handbag marked down from $45 to $11. I also saved $22 on a regular $55 piece of Samsonite luggage. The big-game bargains can be found, you just have to be patient and know when to make your move.

6. If you plan to go in search of the factory outlets and discount stores in your area, grab a friend. Never hunt alone. Some of those factories and bargain barns hang out in hazardous hideaways. Besides, you'll want a second opinion before you buy.

Develop Sales Resistance

Now that I've pumped you full of Adrenalin and you can't wait to get out there and bag the big ones, hold on. Don't venture out without all your faculties. In other words, you must develop mind control.

Bargains like those I've mentioned have been known to affect us in strange ways. We see a bonanza of bargains and it boggles the brains. Our minds reel and we grab up everything on the racks or shelves. *There may never be another chance,* our spellbound minds convince us. It's like biting into a caramel nut roll after a two-week liquid diet. Before you know it, you've gobbled ten, plus a dozen cookies and half the dough. With food we call it overindulgence or "pigging out." With shopping it's called "blowing the budget."

Grabbing all the gusto, when it comes to bargains can wreck your well-planned budget faster than an uninsured medical emergency. So go ahead and find those bargains. Be the big-game bargain hunter and super sales sleuth, but *be careful.* Beat bargain-basement fever with mind control. Here's how:

1. When you see those drastic price reductions and feel your pulse race, STOP! Close your eyes. Take a deep breath and say to yourself, *I am in control. I will remain logical and levelheaded. If I don't, my husband will kill me.* If you don't have a husband say, *If I say yes now, will I still respect myself in the morning?*

2. Now, open your eyes. Check the item over carefully. Much of the merchandise you encounter will be called seconds—the not-yet-ready-for-prime-time line. In some cases, items may be near perfect and reduced because of inventory overload or a clearance of last year's models. Note the workmanship. Is there a sizing problem? Perhaps you'll find a flaw in the material or shipping damage. We found a Lane cedar chest for our daughter, on which we saved $150 because it had suffered a small nick on the back panel during shipping.

3. When you've found the bargain of a lifetime, ask yourself, *Do I really need this? How much am I really saving? Does the quality meet my expectations?*

Don't settle for poor workmanship and materials when you can find quality at the same price or perhaps slightly more. You may end up spending more money in the long run.

Use the same careful deliberation over bargain prices that you would if you were making a $1,000 purchase. Consider whether or not the item and your budget are compatible.

4. Never buy an item you can't return unless it works, it fits, or you are positive you won't develop buyer's remorse. Always check with the seller regarding refund policies. After all, what good is a half-price chicken plucker if it won't pluck chickens. Ask for a demonstration. Likewise, be sure to try on all clothing before you buy. I once bought a designer dress in what I thought was my size. When I brought it home and tried it on, my fashionable dress hung like a potato sack on a gnat.

Well, that about does it. By now you should be a well-equipped bargainer and super sales sleuth. So hit the trail and HAPPY HUNTING!

6
Coupon Clippers and Refunders Extraordinaire-and Those of Us Who Ain't So Hot

AFTER READING THAT LAST CHAPTER ON BARGAIN hunting, you probably got the idea I was a "hot shot." Well, you're right. I can flush out a sale with the confidence and expertise of a bird dog. But, I must confess, when it comes to clipping coupons and refunding, I not only ain't so hot, I'm not even lukewarm.

My skills as a couponer and refunder lie somewhere between the floor and a flea's knees. In fact, the sport makes me almost as enthusiastic as flying into a hurricane or sunbathing in Antarctica.

While I may not qualify for the major leagues, I have a few friends who do. Believe me, they take their game of shopping with coupons and refunds as seriously as the Yankees do baseball.

Refunding in the Majors

I mean it. My friend Linda tells me, "You can always tell a refunder. She's the pack rat who saves everything from the tear strip from her Tide to the empty tube of Crest. Her cupboard is lined with unlabeled cans and cereal boxes that have endured ruthless surgery at the hands of the scissor champ."

I recently caught a pair of these experts at church. Coupon Carla blatantly brought in a sack of empty boxes, labels, and soap wrappers along with a batch of coupons. She passed them on to her friend, Refund Rose. Rose caught the surprise in my eyes and offered an embarrassed explanation.

"We're refunders."

"Oh," I acknowledged, "what's that?"

I was so impressed by her enthusiasm as she explained the refunding process, I invited her home to tell me the whole story.

Within minutes of her arrival, Rose inventoried my pantry and garbage collection. She gasped at my throw-aways.

"Aren't you going to use that refund offer?" She grabbed an empty Rice Krispies box from my trash bag.

"And look at this bagel label," Rose reprimanded, "It's worth a free package of Lender's Bagels."

"I didn't know . . ." I winced.

"Oh! This paper towel wrapper . . . it's a *qualifier.* I've been searching for a month and you were throwing it out." Rose groaned. The experience had obviously shaken her. "It's worth a home run," she finished weakly.

"A what?" I asked. But Rose didn't hear. "Rose," I said gently shaking her shoulders, "snap out of it. You can have the wrapper." I guided her to the living room and offered her a chair. "Before we go any farther, I think you'd better sit down and explain the rules and language of this game. Besides, I think you could use a rest and a cup of coffee."

"Oh, you're right. I'm sorry. I saw all those coupons and refunds and—and I just went to pieces."

"Is this one of the rules—going through your friends' trash for refunds and coupons?"

"It sounds crazy doesn't it?" she admitted. "But, well . . .

you have to be ready. You never know when someone might throw away a qualifier."

"Rose," I interrupted, "you mentioned *qualifier* before and what did you call it . . . a *home run*? What do they mean?"

"I guess I got ahead of myself, didn't I?" Rose admitted. I nodded as she continued. "A qualifier is the part of the product container that the manufacturer requires with a refund application. The refund form tells you what you need to save. Sometimes it's a proof of purchase seal, the net-weight statement, or some other part of the package."

"Oh, yeah!" I acknowledged. "That's simple. Now fill me in on home runs."

"Okay, but I think it might be easier if I explain *double* and *triple plays* first."

"Ah . . . , Rose," I said doubtfully, "are you sure we're still talking about refunds? You're beginning to sound like Howard Cosell."

"You can blame the weird jargon on this magazine," Rose said, handing me her latest copy of *The National Supermarket Shopper*. "According to the editors, a double play is when you find an item on sale and can use a coupon with it. A double savings."

"Oh," I grinned, "I do that all the time, but usually I try to use the store's double coupon."

"Right! But when you do that, it's called a triple play. And," Rose waved the qualifier I'd given her from my garbage bag, "when you can add a refund to that purchase, you have a home run!"

"Wow! I'm impressed, and a little jealous. What got you started in refunding?"

Rose shared how she'd always loved saving money. Any money she receives from her refunding game goes into savings for special gifts and vacations.

"I make from $10 to $50 a month—and that doesn't count what I save on groceries."

"How can you make that much? I tried sending in a refund once. By the time I'd saved enough box tops, the company had gone out of business. I lost my patience and the postage."

"It takes practice. The secret is to have refund offers coming in and going out every day."

"That sounds like a full-time job."

"Not really," advised Rose, "I only spend about five hours a week at it. Refunding is my hobby. I don't really miss the time, because I do most of it while the family's watching television."

Translating Terms

Rose told me she learned the secrets of her refunding trade in *The National Supermarket Shopper.* It has everything you need to become an expert couponer and refunder. The magazine even gives instructions on how to read the magazine. One glance through it and I could understand why. With all the A.C.C.'s, N.A.S.S.'s, POPs, Refund Robins, and traders, I needed a decoder.

You too? Okay, I'll give you a brief review of terms.

- A.C.C.—American Coupon Club.
- N.A.S.S.—National Alliance of Supermarket Shoppers.
- Refund Robins or Shopper's Circles—Refunders and couponers who form small local groups. The members share experiences and information, and trade coupons and refunds.
- POP—Proof of Purchase (i.e., seals, labels, net-weight statements).
- UPC—Universal Product Code, a series of lines with code numbers underneath.
- SMP—Specially Marked Package.
- PP—Purchase Price.
- Traders—Couponers and Refunders who trade by

mail or in person for coupons and refund offers. Traders make it easier to find that particular qualifier you need.

Say for example I have a refund offer from Flatland Mud Facial, Inc., that requires three POPs. Since I don't use the product myself, I'd try to get the qualifiers (POPs) from another trader who uses Mud Facials and give her a qualifier of equal value. By trading labels and box tops, you can fulfill the obligations of the refund offer before it expires and make more money.

These are some of the most common terms. For others you'll want to browse through a copy of *The National Supermarket Shopper.*

Treasure in Trash

Chances are if you're a Toss-it-in-a-drawer-till-tax-time Tilly, you may look on the refund–coupon game skeptically. In fact, Tilly says, "Personally, I look at refunding as a liability. In trying to organize all those refunds, coupons, and rooms full of POPs, I'm liable to *qualify* myself—for a lunacy label."

I must admit, Tilly has a point. It takes considerable determination and dedication to save up all that trash and turn it in for money or free coupons. Rose tells me a bag and pair of scissors are as important to a refunder as a stethoscope and thermometer are to a nurse.

I believe it. Especially after reading an article by Donna Jean and Donna Lynn Bish in the January 1983 issue of *The National Supermarket Shopper.* They tell of ladies who will take every opportunity to hunt for qualifiers. One woman wanted to check out the trash bins of a local nudist camp. She brainstormed and finally figured a way to get in without disrobing. The woman said she'd lost her cat and wanted to look for it.

"Great trash," she told her refunder friends, "but how many weeks in a row can you lose your cat?"

My friend Jane refunds with the zeal of spring love. She finds treasures along roadsides, in the large dumpsters outside restaurants, near rest areas, schools, churches, and campgrounds.

While not all refunders resort to rummaging, many do and find it profitable. Other, less adventuresome players, depend on traders to help them find qualifiers they need and lean more toward the coupon end of the sport.

The refund–coupon game may not seem as exciting to Tilly and me as it does to others, but there is a certain hilarity we all feel in watching the grocery bills shrink.

Coupons Cut Costs

Remember Coupon Carla, Rose's friend? Carla says she spends two to three hours a week preparing her grocery list. She matches manufacturers' coupons and the local grocers' double coupons to the sales items and her grocery list. Carla also sorts through her file of refund offers and decides which products she must buy to fulfill the requirements of the refund deal.

"I have a large coupon selection," says Carla "and am able to use them for about 75 percent of what I buy. It's a lot of work, but worth it because I save at least $100 a month on my grocery bill."

I hear tales of "coupon queens" who dance away from the checkout stand having paid only $1.89 for $97.00 worth of groceries. Most women though simply don't have the time or the energy to indulge in this showy kind of shopping. Among my personal coupon clipper/refunder friends, the average grocery bill drops by about 25 percent with the use of coupons and refund deals. That's not a bad savings. You'll want to read the next chapter on "Super Shopper Tips" for more ways to save at the supermarket.

Will I Ever Reach the Major Leagues?

After my encounter with Rose and Carla, I decided to renew my interest in coupons and refunds. I found a refund offer on a box of Rice Krispies for one free box if I sent in two POPs. Since I only needed one more, I picked up a box on my next shopping trip. My excitement mounted as I grabbed for the scissors. Panic gripped me, as I realized the box held a completely different offer. "Oh," I groaned, "now I'll have to go in search of the right qualifier." *Hmmm,* I wondered, *could it be in my neighbor's trash can?*

I realized then and there I'd never make it to the major leagues. I'd play a little, maybe even get a double or triple, and once in a while get lucky with a home run.

Coupon clipping and refunding can be great sport. But, as with most athletes, we generally focus on one sport and dabble in others. Me? I'm into bargain hunting. Consequently, when it comes to the refund–coupon game, I often strike out. Although I do occasionally make a few great plays, I more often find myself pitching out those terrific offers and letting my friends make the hits.

Of course, that's okay too. To share the wealth I mean. Throwing away those valuable coupons and refund offers is like throwing out cash. Whenever you come across coupons you can't use or refunds you don't intend to cash in on, drop them in a coupon barrel at the store, or pass them on to a friend. They'll love you for it.

Churches are often on the lookout for various POPs. For instance, a Christian school in my area saves POPs from Post cereals. Post offers a program called "Fun 'n Fitness." Through the program, schools can obtain athletic equipment by redeeming the appropriate proof-of-purchase seals. And, how many times do you run across coupons for dog or cat food when you don't have a pet? Even if you can't use them, humane societies can. Call first or they may nab you for littering.

Perhaps like Tillie and myself, you don't feel cut out to be a coupon clipper or refunder. In that case, I'd urge you to practice a little. An occasional play will help keep you in shape should you decide you're ready for the big time if and when you need to tighten your food budget.

7
Super Shoppers Tips

WHETHER YOU PLAY THE LITTLE LEAGUES OR HAVE your heart set on the supermarket shopper championship, you'll want to read through these money-saving, super shopper tips.

1. ***Plan ahead.*** Prepare a shopping list and mark the items on sale and those for which you have coupons. Know before you go which stores have the best prices on the items you need. Many times I make up my grocery list based on the store specials. My weekly menu is also based on specials. To save time and energy, I've devised a shopping form and had the printer run off a batch. The form allows plenty of room and lets even the disorganized housewife become an organized grocery shopper. For a sample see page 73.

I've prepared my form on an 8½-by-11-inch typing sheet. You'll notice that under each of the grocery stores I frequent, I list the store specials that correspond to my "need list." Also, I use a © to identify the items for which I have coupons

STORE #1 *Safeway*	STORE #2 *Fred Meyer*	MENU—SPECIAL ITEMS/REQUESTS	NEED LIST
broccoli 49¢/lb. *hamburger 89¢/lb.* *chicken 63¢/lb.* *Gold Medal (unbleached)* *roast beef 1.98 lb.* *carrots 3 lb bag/99¢* *red snapper 1.89 lb*	*margarine 2/1.00* *Skippy Peanut Butter © DC* *eggs 59¢/doz.* *Windex 1.69 © DC* *Wheaties 89¢ © DC* *Moist Meals ©* *Lender's Bagels 89¢ © DC* **orange juice 12oz 78¢* *ice cream 79¢* *(half gal.)* *Colby Cheddar 2 lb. 4.59* *tuna 79¢*	*special dishes* *stir-fried veg.* *zucchini, chinese* *mushrooms* *meat sauce* *mushrooms* *olives*	*milk* *lettuce* *fresh veg.* *fruit* *margarine* *peanut butter* *flour* *Windex* *toilet paper* *onions* *cereal* *cat food* *bagels* *juice* *cream cheese* *meat* *fish* *lentils*
STORE #3 *Keil's*	STORE #4 *Thriftway*	MISC. NOTES *Food Warehouse*	
Miracle Whip (32 oz) 89¢	*Northern toilet* *tissue 89¢ ©* *yellow onions 39¢ lb.* **orange juice (12 oz) 67¢* *green beans 2 cans/79¢*	*(Shop here first and compare prices — they take other store's double coupons—up to 5.)*	

and a DC to show items I can purchase using the store's double coupons. I also include a menu column for specialty items or family request items. We usually start our shopping at a discount or U-Mark-it store. With the list, I can readily see how their prices compare with those of the other stores on my list. Many times I end up buying nearly all my groceries at the U-Mark-it because the prices run the same or less, and this particular store accepts all the other supermarkets' double coupons.

In addition to this super shopping form, you'll need an envelope for your coupons. Clip together all the coupons you'll be using at each store. In other words, you'll have a batch for Safeway, one for A&P, and so on. Slip a small piece of paper with the store's name on it with each batch so you won't get them mixed up.

A close friend, Margo, uses a master grocery list. She sat down one day and typed out a list of all the items she uses. When she runs out of an item or runs low, she yellow-lines or checks that product on a copy of her master grocery list. For a sample of Margo's list, see page 75.

2. ***Stick to your list.*** Try to avoid buying items you don't have on your list. Stores love to entice you with walking, life-size pizzas, or Twinkies, or some weirdo squeezing toilet paper. Turning an impulse buyer loose in a grocery store is like locking up a sugar addict in a candy factory. What chance does she have? None. But does the store care? No! They just keep coming up with more and more irresistible packaging and ways to convince me I can't live another two hours unless I buy their product. Which brings me to another tip.

3. ***Never shop hungry.*** And don't bring your ravenous husband or kids. Actually, it's better if you shop alone, on a full stomach. I learned this truth after watching my grocery bill zoom over the $150 mark while shopping

Fresh fruits & veggies

- tomatoes
- lettuce
- celery
- onions
- green peppers
- potatoes
- carrots
- cabbage
- oranges
- apples
- bananas
- grapes
- pineapple
- strawberries
- peaches

Dairy products

- milk
- cream
- buttermilk
- cheddar cheese
- lite cheese
- process cheese slices
- cottage cheese
- butter
- margarine
- eggs
- sour cream

Meat

- hamburger
- steak
- roast beef
- pork chops
- ham
- bacon
- sausage
- chicken
- turkey
- bologna
- corned beef
- tuna

Pasta

- rice
- navy beans
- spaghetti
- macaroni
- popcorn

Cleaning Agents

- ammonia
- Borax
- bleach
- laundry det.
- liq. dish det.
- fabric softener
- dish washer det.
- washing soda
- Comet

Cereal & Bread

- corn flakes
- Cheerios
- Rice Krispies
- Corn Chex
- Rice Chex
- Wheat Chex
- Kix
- Grape Nuts
- Spoon Size Shredded Wheat
- oatmeal
- Cream of Wheat
- tapioca
- Measure-up
- whole wheat
- bagels
- hamb-buns
- hot dog buns
- crackers

Staples

- flour
- g. sugar
- brown sugar
- powdered sugar
- salt
- molasses
- table syrup
- corn syrup
- raisins
- corn starch
- yeast
- nuts
- cocoa
- unsweet choc.
- coffee
- tea
- Nestles Quik
- peanut butter
- Miracle Whip
- catsup
- mustard
- tartar sauce
- dill pickles
- tomato sauce
- tomato soup
- chicken noodle
- cream soup
- pork & beans
- canned chili
- spaghetti mix
- corn
- peas
- beans
- carrots
- mushrooms
- olives
- beef bouillon
- chili beans
- Crisco oil

Fruit cocktail

- peaches
- pears
- cherries
- apples
- pineapple

Spices

- vanilla ex.
- almond ex.
- cinnamon
- ginger
- nutmeg
- allspice
- cloves

Dog & cat food

Paper products

- paper plates
- paper cups
- napkins
- toilet paper
- paper towels
- sanitary supplies
- aluminum foil
- Saran Wrap
- Ziploc bags
- garbage bags
  - small
  - med.
  - large
- vacuum cleaner bags (Hoover type A)
- shampoo
- conditioner
- toothpaste
- toothbrushes
- deodorant
- coffee filters

with my teenage son. I'd just fed him, but with him it didn't matter.

"How do you expect me to grow if you don't keep frozen pizzas in the house? Why don't you get some of these fish sticks and chicken snacks, then when you're at work, I won't starve," Dave argued. "We're out of ice cream—six gallons okay?"

By the time the shopping trip ended, I was not only broke, I'd been sent on so many guilt trips I had jet lag.

4. ***Comparison shop.*** This applies to groceries as well as clothing and household items. Look over the unit prices before you buy. Unit price is that computer readout located below each item on the shelf. It tells you how much per pound or ounce (unit) you are paying for the product. Even if you plan to use a coupon, the price of an off brand may be less than your coupon item.

Check out the lower shelves. Lower-priced products tend to linger there. Also, look over and try a few plain-label brands. You may have to hunt around to find the best combination of quality and price, but eventually, you'll know which of the less-expensive brands you can trust.

5. ***Avoid buying processed food.*** For example, if you bought a can of ready-made frosting with a coupon and saved 50 percent it would still cost you five times more than the sugar, butter, and milk you use in making the frosting from scratch. Make your own whenever possible. See Part II, "The Money Eaters," for more information on convenience foods.

6. ***Be a supermarket hopper only if it pays.*** Consider your transportation costs before you drive all over town to take advantage of specials. Your savings should come to more than the costs of running your car.

7. ***Take a cooler.*** Is grocery shopping an all-day affair for you? Does the ice cream you got at store #1 turn into tire soup in your trunk by the time you reach store #4? Protect all those frozen foods by bringing along a cooler with ice.

8. ***Frequent warehouses, U-Mark-its, and manufacturers' outlets.*** Just as you can find some great buys on nonfood items at discount stores, you can find groceries at cut-rate, no-fancy-stuff prices as well. You may have to mark your own packages and bag your own groceries and forgo the song-and-dance routine of "Bobby Bagle" and "Carmella Cream Cheese." Impulse buyers will feel safer in this no-fluff environment.

9. ***Stock up.*** Whenever possible, buy in bulk. Stock up on staples you use regularly when they are on sale or when you shop the discount stores. Items like paper towels, tomatoes, toilet paper, flour, sugar, vegetables, shortening—anything you know you will use. Unfortunately, padding your pantry costs money. Perhaps you can't afford to buy many items in bulk, but at least once a month, buy a case or large quantity of one or two items. You will also need the storage space for case or bulk buying. You can definitely save money when you buy in quantity. However, don't fret if you've neither the money nor the space. There are other ways you can save.

10. ***Save a bundle on paper products by buying less.*** If you shop, you know the cost of paper products runs higher than skyrockets on the Fourth of July. Cut your costs drastically by using scraps of material to make cloth napkins. Use newspapers rather than paper towels to clean your windows. Try going back to cloth diapers rather than Pampers. Some new mothers I've talked with lately think of disposable diapers as a necessity. Actually, disposables create a waste problem and in many instances cause skin allergies and severe diaper rash. As a veteran mother dedicated to cloth diapers, I can assure you they don't take too much time and they are better for baby. (Hint for Mom: Use a vinegar rinse, about one cup vinegar in second rinse, on diapers. Vinegar cuts the ammonia in baby's urine and helps reduce diaper rash. For more advice about diaper rash and other rashes, see my book for parents, *The Care & Feeding of Sick Kids*).

11. ***Take advantage of sales, coupons, double coupons, and refunds whenever you can.*** Don't be discouraged if you can't compete with those coupon queens, paying only 98¢ for $150 worth of groceries. Be happy where you are. Rejoice when you can save 50¢ or even a dime. Remember to save enormous sums of money at the checkout stand takes weeks and months of collecting coupons and refund deals. And, while we're not all cut out to be coupon queens, we can all cut out coupons and cut our costs by being wise shoppers.

12. ***"Do all things without grumbling . . ."*** (Philippians 2:14 RSV). *Surely that can't mean grocery shopping. It's my most unfavorite thing to do.* If those are your thoughts, I understand. Grocery shopping has about as much appeal as diving into a shark-infested swimming pool. It's brutal—a jungle—a savage world of hit-and-run grocery carts, long checkout lines, no bathroom, and color-coded, designed-with-you-in-mind products screaming, "Buy me! Buy me!" When you finally break out, you face a husband who can't understand why you look like you've just run the Boston Marathon.

About the only way I can come away from a shopping trip with a smile is when I've bought only what I went for and spent less than I budgeted. I may still look bedraggled as a marathon runner, but the grumbling vanishes behind the glow of winning.

You need confidence and willpower to survive supermarket shopping and save money, but it can be done. The amount of money you save on groceries is directly related to the time you spend in preparation.

In the following chapter you'll learn about a money-saving skill that requires little time and a sharp mind.

8

How to Haggle and Be a Heroine

"'UTTERLY WORTHLESS!' SAYS THE BUYER AS HE HAGGLES over the price. But afterwards he brags about his bargain!" (Proverbs 20:14 TLB)

As you see, haggling, also known as dickering or higgling, has been an inflation-beating method of economy-minded buyers since biblical times. Unfortunately, many consumers today think of haggling as offensive, rude, distasteful, and not worth the bother. And, let's face it, there are many stores where one simply doesn't quibble about the price.

However, there are still merchants who drop their prices before you even have a chance to ask. Here's where we can practice and gain expertise in the art of haggling.

Perhaps you're objecting, "But I don't want to be a haggler, a higgler, or even a dickerer. They sound about as feminine as a football game. Isn't haggling an insult to the seller? Besides I—I'm too shy."

Good points. I don't like the names either. So, why don't we call ourselves *negotiators?* I can live with that. Negotiators discuss terms and come to mutual agreements with others. Negotiating doesn't have to be an insult. In fact, if the merchant is insulted in the process, you have made an error in your technique.

I'm Too Shy

As to shyness, I understand. Negotiating has always been one of our family's biggest money-savers. My husband is the expert. In the twenty years we've been married, thanks to my negotiating mate, we've never paid the asking price on any appliance (large or small), car, furniture, or house. We usually manage to come away with a great bargain, satisfied with both the quality and the price.

Personally, I took a dim view of negotiating in the earlier years of our marriage. I thought what the sticker said was fair and lawful and to question it would be mutinous. My logic? Why would anyone want to go through the trouble of pricing something if it wasn't right? Can you imagine my embarrassment on one of our first shopping trips for furniture when Ron spotted an easy chair and said to the salesman, "I'll give you $40 for it."

I couldn't believe he'd said that. I mean the price tag clearly read $60. The *nerve* of some people. I backed away from the scene and pretended not to know him. Ever had the feeling?

What really cinched it was when the seller argued, "What do you mean $40? It's already discounted at $60."

"I knew it," I mumbled, as I slunk another foot from the action.

Ron looked over the chair with the scrutiny of a sergeant looking over his new recruits. "Forty-five dollars cash. That's my final offer."

I bit the back of my hand and closed my eyes, expecting to see the manager escort my brash husband out the door.

"Sold!" declared the seller.

"What?" I gasped and stared at the salesman. I inched my way back to Ron's side. "You mean it's ours? For $45?" My embarrassment turned to joy as we carried our prize out of the store.

Lesson 1: Trust your haggling husband.

Lesson 2: The value merchants stick on their merchandise does not necessarily reflect the true value.

Lesson 3: Many sellers inflate prices because they expect to negotiate.

Some Folks Haggle, Some Folks Don't

I learned lesson 3 above from a guy who runs a discount builders' supply. After a short haggling session with me, the older gentleman confessed, "To tell you the truth, I'm glad you talked me down. I feel guilty and a little red-faced when folks come in here and buy this stuff without questioning the price."

Although most people wouldn't admit it, there are many shops where some form of negotiation is expected. You'll find this especially true in "used" or antique stores, car salesrooms and lots, flea markets, garage sales, and furniture, carpeting, and appliance stores.

Usually, clothing stores and supermarkets have set prices, although it is possible to negotiate on outdated or damaged goods. How do I know? Listen, you don't live twenty years with a haggling hero without having some tricks of the trade rub off on you.

At any rate let's get back to "nonnegotiable" stores. While shopping at Vancouver Mall, I found a blouse I'd been wanting. The dusty rose perfectly matched my suit. Unfortunately, one of the buttons was missing. There were others like it, but only that one in my color. Since it was already on sale, I hesitated asking for compensation because of the button.

Then I noticed the other sale blouses were without flaws. *I'll do it!* I took a deep breath and courageously confronted the manager.

"I love this blouse," I admitted, "but it's the only one in dusty rose and there's a button missing. I'll probably have to replace all of them since a match is unlikely. Would you consider discounting it for me?"

She agreed to a 20 percent discount off the marked sale price.

Lesson 4: You can negotiate the price of practically anything—anywhere.

Cash In on the Competition

While comparison shopping in itself saves cash, you can often up the savings by cool and clever negotiations. Suppose you found a quality dining room set in store #1, which is only a couple of miles from your home. In your comparison shopping you find the identical set for $150 less, but store #2 is forty-five miles round trip from your home. Naturally, you'd rather save yourself a return trip to store #2, so you negotiate with store #1. Since many stores advertise competitive pricing, your chances of success are as great as catching a trout on opening day.

I cashed in on store-to-store competition the last time I bought a pair of shoes. Heels Unlimited had a pair of Soulars on sale for $36. They weren't quite the color I had in mind, so the search continued. Comparison shopping landed me in front of a pair of maroon Soulars. Unfortunately, at the Bootery they cost $45.

As I tried them on and walked about, I casually remarked, "Nice fit. But did you know that Heels Unlimited has them on sale for $36?" Once I had his attention I sighed and said, "Of course I like this color a little better, but for $9 difference I could probably live with brown."

"We'll meet Heels' price," he reflected. "Just a second while I verify the sale."

I didn't exactly save more money by buying my shoes at the last store. But I did save energy by not making a return trip, and I did get the color best suited to my wardrobe and that's worth more than cash.

Lesson 5: Many stores will meet the competitive sale prices asked in other stores.

Negotiating With Tact

Wherever you choose to negotiate, there is one lesson that stands above all the others.

Lesson 6: Be understanding and sensitive to the seller. Use tact. "A gentle answer turns away wrath, but a harsh word stirs up anger" (Proverbs 15:1 NASB).

Having been on both sides of the bargaining table, I can attest to the value of this lesson. At one of my latest art sales, a woman cruelly insulted me and my craft by offering plastic-ware prices for handcrafted pottery. The haggler made the mistake of not knowing the value or work involved in the art pieces she wanted to buy. She made the same mistake with a fellow craftsman who sold beautiful hand-carved wood sculpture.

I'm not saying that it's inappropriate to negotiate prices with artists. By all means do. Most of us don't mind at all. But please know the craft and comparable values before making an offer. In all honesty, I would rather give away my work to someone who appreciates the value than sell at an unworthy price.

In fact, I did just that at a Christmas sale. One woman had walked by my table several times. Each time she stopped and picked up one of my $8.50 honey pots. She finally asked me, "Do you have any like this . . . a second maybe that I could buy for $4?"

"I'm sorry, I don't," I told her and showed her some pieces in her price range. We talked at length about the art of pottery and her genuine interest warmed me. She did find a $4 piece, but her eyes kept moving longingly to the honey pot. I couldn't resist. Along with her purchase I wrapped up the honey pot topped with a tiny, hand-sculpted bear and gave it to her.

"I know you'll give it a good home," I explained. From the joy in her eyes I knew we were both satisfied customers.

The Bogey Tactic

In "The Fine Art of Getting the Price Down on Practically Anything" (*Woman's Day*, September 2, 1980), Susan Fletcher writes about the "bogey tactic." That's where you blame someone or something other than your good sense on the high price problem. "Husbands make wonderful bogeys," Susan says, "so do budgets, new homes, new babies—anything that restricts your cash flow."

Suppose you've fallen in love with a four-foot stuffed version of a koala bear. "It would be a perfect complement to my jungle decor," you sigh, "but my husband and my budget would go ape over the price tag." Continue to drool for a few minutes. The salesman should realize by now that if he or she doesn't bring down the price so you can buy it, you will undoubtedly go into severe depression. If you were a salesperson would you like to have that hanging over your head?

If after your genuine performance the seller resists, muster up your most baleful expression and make eye contact. Sigh audibly. Turn away slowly with your head hung and start to leave. Listen carefully, the merchant may make an offer. After all, four-foot koala bears may not be selling well this season.

If this ploy gets you nowhere and you still want that bear, make an offer. You may not always get what you want, but don't be afraid to ask. Keep your negotiations on friendly terms.

Be a Haggling Hero and Heroine Team

Another tip from Susan's article is that you "work as a team with your husband or a friend." When I read her advice I had to chuckle. Ron and I had been a negotiating team for years and didn't even realize it.

For example, I remember when we finally found the new furniture we wanted. I panted over the furniture, while Ron played the villain. I drooled over the color and dreamed about floor plans. Ron scratched his head and asked me, "Are you sure this is what you want? That set down at Newton's is $300 less."

About this time the salesman whipped out his notebook and calculated that, yes, he could come down $300. After a brief negotiation session, they came to terms, and the furniture came to live at our house.

Not all of our teamwork produced bumper crops. There were times I went away pouting. And Ron didn't always play the villain. Sometimes, we turned the roles around and I played the part of the unwilling spouse.

The Haggle Hero Meets His Match

Our culture is not, as a whole, attuned to dickering. There are some places however, like Saudi Arabia, where the art is taught in early childhood as a way of life.

It was with one such person that my haggle hero husband met his match. This time we were the sellers. Back in our college days, we owned a '54 Plymouth that we needed to sell so we could eat. Ron tacked up a notice: "1954 Plymouth, 2-door, good condition—$300."

An exchange student from Saudi Arabia contacted us. After seeing the car and talking to Ron, he made a firm offer.

"One hundred dollar!"

"It's worth at least $300. The car's in really good shape," Ron replied.

"One hundred dollar!"

"That's ridiculous. I'll tell you what. I'll sell it to you for $250. No less," Ron stated.

"One hundred dollar!"

Negotiations were *not* going well. The student left and returned four days later. "One-hundred-twenty-five dollar!" he offered.

Ron tried to explain that the car was worth $300, but his words missed their mark. "Okay," Ron felt himself sinking, "I'll take $225."

"One-hundred-fifty dollar!"

Whether it was hunger or frustration that finally broke Ron's will, I'm not sure. All I know is, he agreed. He said, "I've been haggled by one of the best."

Ron hadn't entirely lost face in the deal. The Arab told him he considered Ron the expert for negotiating him up $50 over his original offer.

Negotiate. It's fun and practical and certainly can save you a bundle. Don't feel intimidated. You should feel free to negotiate for the best and fairest price. As a consumer it is your right to question prices and the worth of a product.

Just remember to be friendly and praise the product. This way you'll most likely end up with a smile and a little extra money in your pocket. No time or special talents are required for this money-saving tool. To negotiate, all you need are the incentive, a joyful, pleasant attitude, and a desire for the best buy.

9
Barter Basics

BY NOW YOU SHOULD BE SAVING BUNDLES BY USING all those ideas on how to haggle, clip coupons, refund, and bargain hunt. Maybe you feel the money-saving supply store is about exhausted. Not so. In fact, we've barely tapped the surface. The real gems lay in this chapter on barter and chapter 10 on the do-it-yourselfer.

I'm especially excited about barter because with it you save money by not spending money.

Bartering, in case you're unfamiliar with the term, has been an accepted rate of exchange since . . . well, since Eve! Anyway it's been around a long time. Or, perhaps you recognize it better if we call it swapping or horse-trading. It means trading labor or goods without using money.

After money came on the scene as the main rate of exchange, barter practically sank out of sight. But today, with money as fleeting as the United States Navy, barter is back and seaworthy as the U.S. Enterprise.

These days people trade everything. Gardeners swap tomatoes for onions. Farmers trade hay for ham. Lawyers exchange their brains for a builder's brawn. Doctors even get in on the barter act. A plumber discussing surgery with his urologist said, "You fix my plumbing and I'll fix yours." That's called professional bartering.

With so many people getting into bartering, the process can become extremely complicated, bureaucratic, and impersonal.

To illustrate this, take a look at the various ways barter is used and misused in the United States.

The One-on-One

Individual barter is a simple system of equal trade between friends or neighbors. For example, not long ago I traded several pieces of pottery for my friend's sewing skills. Ellen agreed to complete a suit and blouse I had cut out several months before.

My friend Lois made an excellent swap last fall. She noticed a walnut tree in her neighbors' yard. Knowing the neighbors were elderly and unable to harvest the nuts, she made them an offer.

"I'll pick all your walnuts if you'll let me have a few pounds for cooking this winter."

"Help yourself," the couple agreed. "You can have all but ten pounds. That's all we need."

Lois's bartering helped her neighbors and brought her all the walnuts she needed.

The other day my brother asked me if he could pick out a gift from my pottery studio. He chose a set of mugs.

"I don't have any money to pay for these. Can I make you something?" he asked.

"No," I smiled, "but you can bring me a couple steelhead." (My brother catches all those "big ones" that usually get away.)

"Sure!" he grinned. Since fishing is his favorite hobby, I knew we'd both made an equitable trade.

Individual bartering brings friends and neighbors together as they share their crafts and skills. The simplicity and warmth of a friendly swap can be extended to include more than a one-on-one relationship. It can encompass a whole neighborhood or community.

Community Barter

A community barter usually exists in the form of a co-op, where people pool their resources. One example that comes to mind is a baby-sitting co-op that my friend Cheryl belongs to. A group of six mothers got together and set up a system where they trade baby-sitting time. In order to avoid time-consuming paperwork, each mother is given a roll of fifty tickets. Each ticket buys one hour of baby-sitting time.

If Cheryl leaves her toddler at Mary's house for three hours, she pays Mary with three tickets. Great system. Maybe you're wondering what happens when Cheryl uses all her tickets. That's simple, she gets more. But there's a catch. The only way Cheryl can replenish her ticket supply is to baby-sit for Mary or another member of the co-op.

Community barter takes place whenever you have several swappers involved. Another example would be a garden swap. Suppose you have a ton of carrots, Martha down the street is overrun with tomatoes, Pete planted enough potatoes to feed your teenagers for two years, and Harvey, in his first green thumb project, underestimated the potential proliferation of zucchini.

The only logical thing to do, in order to prevent a winter of boring reruns, is pool resources—swap. And variety will once again be acclaimed life's spice.

Branching farther along in the barter business we find an extension of the community barter—the barter exchange.

The Barter Exchange

The barter exchange differs from co-ops and community groups in that there are usually more people involved. Also, in an exchange, you may be dealing with strangers. Exchanges are usually set up by individuals or groups who want to bring traders together. These nonprofit organizations provide a service to people in the community who might have difficulty locating a barter partner on their own.

Say for instance, Jane wanted to trade her pet alligator for an affectionate boa constrictor. Since both items seldom top the most-wanted list, finding a swap mate might be of help. Jane lists her needs with the exchange and waits for an alligator lover who's fed up with her boa.

All of these forms of barter have proven respectable and profitable. Most of the time, simple swaps between people include honesty as well as goods and services. But not all barter reeks of honesty. In fact this next method of barter can leave you wondering what happened to your shirt.

Horse-trade for Fun and Profit

Horse traders work hard at their trade. Ever met one? A bona fide horse trader dresses to deliberately put himself at an advantage. The more bedraggled the appearance, the better. Swapping with one will probably give you more enjoyment than a three-day beach retreat. You may come away with a pile of junk worth five times less than what you brought to trade. But the tour through Trader Tom's treasures and an earful of Tom's trading tales will keep your funny bone tickled for days. When you finally realize you've been had, you'll probably shrug your shoulders and chalk it up to experience.

Horse-trading, also called swapping-up, doesn't have to be an I-win, you-lose situation. Say for example you own a Rototiller. The only problem is, you've recently moved into an apartment—on the thirteenth floor. How much is that Rototiller worth to you? A side of beef? A few dozen eggs? A bushel or two of vegetables from the farm? Maybe after a few months of tripping over the motorized shovel you're tempted to pay someone to take it away.

Consequently, the money value may not be as important in a trade as usefulness. Remember though, if you're concerned about making a fair-value trade, avoid the expert horse trader who'll give you the fun and keep the profit.

And speaking of profit, this final branch of the barter tree is definitely out to make one.

Barter Clubs

Anyone can join a barter club or organization—for a price. In her book *What'll You Take For It?*, Annie Proulx warns us about the lack of regulations and guidelines for barter clubs. "Anyone can start a barter club out of his hat," she says, "and be free to issue scrip, credits, zingtwiddles, or whatever form of tender he wishes, and free to draw up simple or complicated and tricky rules that force members to play the swapping game his way only."

Through some of the computer-processed barter organizations you can make trades for practically everything. In some cases this wide range of accessibility can help you find that perfect trade. However, there are dangers. Not all barter clubs can claim honesty. Check out the barter club for credibility and shallowness before you dive into the barter pool.

Another problem these large-scale clubs stirred up involves the IRS. With big business cutting in on barter profits, Uncle Sam has taken a renewed interest in barter.

"You Mean They'd Tax My Traded Turnips?"

Did you know that if the Internal Revenue Service wanted to, they could collect taxes on all forms of barter? When I first read the IRS ruling on barter, I said, "What? You mean they'd tax my traded turnips?"

"We could," declared the tax man who answered the IRS information number.

"How long has the IRS been interested in bartering?" I asked, having simmered down from my original boiling point.

"The law has always stated that, legally, you must declare bartering as a source of income or expense."

"Oh," I frowned. "Everything?"

"Nearly," he answered. "You must declare labor traded for labor or goods. If you work for someone and receive equal labor back, both parties must declare an income value."

"What about my turnips?"

"Trading for produce or goods of equal value, which is most often done between friends and neighbors, usually has no tax implications."

The IRS used to take little or no interest in barter. But, with the advent of the mega-barter industry, they've been losing too much revenue to let it slide.

"A recent IRS study indicates that in one year a whopping $75 billion of legally earned income was simply not reported, with a tax loss estimated at $13 to $17 billion. Barter was most frequently named the villain," says Annie Proulx in her barter book.

You can bet Uncle Sam does not take kindly to such large losses. Consequently, the big bartering organizations must provide the IRS with a list of participants and their bartering record on demand.

But don't let government's renewed interest in trade spoil your fun. Enjoy! Try your hand at bartering, but keep it simple—between friends and neighbors. It's fun and provides quality services, fresh conversations, and goodwill.

So barter. Keep records. Then, render unto Uncle Sam what is Uncle Sam's—and nothing more.

affirmative response suggests you forget self and let someone else do it for you. (Try barter instead.)

	Yes	?	No
1. Does the mass of metal under your car's hood remind you of a hostile alien from the planet "Grime"?	☐	☐	☐
2. Could you add oil, brake fluid, and window washer without ending up with greasy windshield, water on the brake drum, and frozen pistons, not to mention a dead car?	☐	☐	☐
3. Do you start projects and never finish them?	☐	☐	☐
4. If someone blessed you with a hundred "round-to-its" would you still have projects that you never got around to?	☐	☐	☐
5. Do you have half an afghan stuffed in the back of your spare closet?	☐	☐	☐
6. Is the last dress you cut out still waiting for the styles to change—for the third time?	☐	☐	☐
7. Do you have drawers full of materials or other craft supplies longing for a creator to make something out of them?	☐	☐	☐
8. Does your patience, time, and money run out before your projects end?	☐	☐	☐

Not everyone was created with the ability to do it all themselves. While some women may want to rebuild the engine of their '47 Chevy, others may find comfort and cost efficiency in building a fence. Me? I'll stick to constructing a wardrobe and producing pottery. Over the years I've found, by trial and error (mostly error), there are some projects my Creator never meant for me to do. Woodworking is one of them.

Nails never worked well for me. I can't say as I blame them. How useful would you be if someone beat you on the head till you bent, straightened you with a crowbar, and bent you again. My husband once fired me as a carpenter. I kept throwing nails away because they were facing the wrong way. With me at the hammer even the good nails never quite hit their mark.

We all have our specialties, and there are many areas where we can learn do-it-yourself skills. Fortunately, there are books that tell us how to do everything. Before we embark on a do-it-yourself project, we should ask ourselves these questions.

- Do I know what I'm doing?
- Considering the cost of materials and the time involved, am I really saving money?
- Is this a project I am meant to do, or am I feeling pressured because *everyone else* is doing it?

How Doing It Yourself Can Save You Money

Jan, a single parent, learned through her farmer father, about the rewards of do-it-yourself auto mechanics. Jan changes the oil, brake fluid, and even does minor engine repairs and maintenance.

Local colleges teach classes in auto repair and maintenance. Auto manufacturers publish booklets on how to take care of their kind of car. Learn as much as you want to. Maybe you want to be able to pull out the carburetor and put it back together—right. Or, you might just want to learn to change a tire in an emergency, or pump your own gas. You don't have to go to extremes to save a little money on your gas guzzler, but every tinker helps.

For $28 worth of materials, I sewed a four-piece wool suit for my daughter, Caryl. We saved $102 over a comparative value. Doing it yourself and saving means you must shop around for the best buys on materials, calculate the estimated cost, and compare your figures with those of similar ready-made products.

Many times I have made my estimations only to find a sale item for less. It would be only fair to include in your estimations the time element. How much is your time worth? Could you have it done or purchase a ready-made product for less than what you can make at your job? Of course if the do-it-yourself project is a hobby, time spent wouldn't be a factor.

Do-it-yourselfers, like barterers, negotiators, super shoppers, couponers and refunders, bargain hunters, and super sleuths, can and do save hundreds, perhaps even thousands of dollars a year. They simply use one or a combination of several money-saving methods we've discussed in this section.

You've probably already dabbled in some. I've found that homemakers, especially those of us who lack funds, can be extremely resourceful. Hopefully, some of these ideas will help you sharpen your money-saving skills. We need all the help we can get to chip away at the inflation that threatens to destroy our budgets.

Remember, money saved is money managed. Even if you aren't the head money manager of the family, you can do your part in the team effort by applying these principles to strengthen your buying power.

As we leave our section on saving money and move on to making extra money through talents and treasures, I'd like to share a final thought. A friend recently gave me a new thought about money.

"When you make various purchases," Pam said, "don't think of yourself as spending money. Rather, approach the matter as you would a transaction where you sell your money to the merchant in exchange for merchandise. By changing your thought process about your money tool, you will always want to get the most product for the money you sell."

11

Sharing the Load

"SAVE MONEY—SHOWER WITH A FRIEND." OR WAS IT, "Save water. . ."? Oh well, no matter. Remember that old saying, whatever it was? It came at about the time *inflation* became as common a household word as *soap*. Of course, showering with a friend might raise a few eyebrows, unless your friend is your mate—then it could be fun. But, as to saving money or water? I don't know about you, but when I shower with my husband, saving water and money concern me about as much as what to wear.

Co-showering mightn't relieve your financial burdens, but there are many ways in which cooperating with friends can ease the money crunch.

Food Co-ops

Food co-ops have blossomed up in our area like crocuses after a winter thaw. Several of my friends take advantage of the price reductions co-ops offer. In case you haven't heard of a food co-op, the ground rules are basic. The co-op consists of a group of people who pool their grocery lists so they can buy their food from distributors in bulk quantities. Buying in bulk often brings drastic price reductions.

"Well," you may be asking, "if food co-ops are really so great why doesn't everyone do it? We could eliminate supermarkets."

Good question. Along with the obvious benefits, there come a few complications. Each participant in the co-op must take a turn at picking up the food order, distributing it to the various group members, and collecting the money for the venture.

Consequently, a question to ask yourself before you get involved with food co-ops is, *Do I have the time to act as a distributor and the space for a food warehouse?* Unfortunately, I have neither. I've placed the food co-op on my future goal list for when I become the perfect 10 on the organization scale. Through my friends I have been able to pick up a few items, like ten pounds of cashews (raw) for $1.89 a pound. These delicacies usually run about $3.69 retail. I've also bought ten-pound quantities of Danish Havarti and cheddar cheese at savings of over a dollar a pound.

Another question you need to ask yourself before going co-op on food is this: *How much do I actually save after the co-op fees, sales tax, car expenses for travel time, and my time in picking up and splitting the orders.*

While most cooperative groups provide a neighborhood service between friends, unfortunately, some have sprung up out of greed. Before you join a food club or co-op, check credentials. Is someone giving a sales pitch and offering you a simplistic, get-rich-quick scheme? Question their motives and get an account of any money you are required to pay. The Apostle Paul tells us in Ephesians 5:6, "Let no one deceive you with empty words . . ." (RSV).

I don't mean to deter you from food co-ops. In fact, my

friends belong to an excellent group. One woman, who formulated and runs the group, has a business license that allows her to buy from wholesalers. She is paid a 10 percent fee of whatever amount is ordered. This fee must cover her phone calls, travel, and accounting. In this particular group there are two women who see that the orders are in and the money is collected. In other co-ops this burden may be shared. As far as I'm concerned 10 percent is a small price to pay for such dedicated and efficient organization.

By the way, this particular food co-op is the one I intend to join when I get around to it. A bonus in my friends' co-op is that it's all natural food. And, speaking of natural food, how about co-operating a garden?

Car Pools

Do you commute? Do you act as chauffeur along with all your other jobs? Car pooling is another great way to share the load and save money. When five or six people commute to the same place, why go your separate ways?

Cars are expensive. Sometimes we forget just how much they actually cost. In chapter 2 I mentioned a book by George and Marjean Fooshee—*You Can Beat the Money Squeeze.* In it the authors give a factual account of what it really costs to operate that driving necessity, the automobile. According to George and Marjean, the gas cost is only a minor expense to car owners. "For instance," the book reads, "when you put $12 of gas in your tank, did you also put aside $40.45 for those other certain expenses."

"Forty dollars," I choked. Then I read on. These other expenses include insurance, taxes, repairs, maintenance, and—eventually—car replacement. The Fooshees figured out exactly what it costs to run a car per year and came up with an astounding figure of $.259 per mile. Which, if you drive 12,000 miles a year comes to $3,108.

With facts and figures like that, we don't need much more

incentive to cooperate with friends and neighbors in reducing the car expenses. Hey . . . how about co-owning the car?

Pool Tools, Lawnmowers, and . . .

Can you imagine what sort of life a lawnmower leads? Or a hedge clipper? How would you feel if you were used only once a week or once every six months? What a lonely life—and useless.

And, we have the power to end all that loneliness, simply by sharing these seldom-used tools with our neighbors. Sure, I'll admit sometimes it's a hassle, so is tripping over the used-once-a-year chain saw, or a biyearly hedge clipper, or, of course, the weekly lawnmower stored in your garage.

Naturally, this community sharing project requires consideration for and from all the partners. Returning a dull chain saw or lawnmower is like exchanging a rotten egg for a fresh one. Bad taste—very bad taste.

Co-habitation

Relax. I'm not going to suggest you go join a commune or anything like that. But, I am going to suggest sharing the load of owning or renting a home and/or property.

Sharing an apartment or home isn't reserved for single gals. In fact, of late, I'm seeing more and more couples as well as single-parent families pool together to buy a multifamily dwelling or home. These families work together to pay rent or mortgages, utilities, and sometimes even grocery bills.

Problems? Certainly, what group of people don't have some problems? In many cases, however, home sharers end up with more benefits than Blue Cross.

A friend, Jill, who is single and a mother of two, agrees. "I never could have afforded to keep our home if it hadn't been for Sharon," Jill explained.

Sharon, mother of three, had been divorced three years.

The two women met at a singles' ministry conference. As they discussed problems of running a household alone, the idea struck—why not combine forces. They did.

"Our kids are like brothers and sisters," Jill said. "Sometimes I think they forget which of us is their real mother, and I forget who belongs to me."

"What about the household chores?" I asked. "Ever fight over who cooks or how cupboards are arranged? Every once in a while my kids or husband decide to be helpful and rearrange the cupboards. I appreciate the help, but not in my kitchen. What I really wish they'd rearrange are their clothes—from the bedroom floor to their closets."

"Fortunately," Sharon grinned, "we've never had the 'my kitchen' syndrome. We switch the chores weekly. When it's Jill's turn to cook, I feel like I have a maid."

Co-habitation can work. You'll need to draw up a contract to avoid problems with who pays for what, when, and how. Make certain you are compatible. For example, if you don't smoke, don't room with a smoker, especially if you have smoke allergies.

Jill says, "Sharon and I are both Christians. We have similar life-styles. That's important in house sharing."

"Another important aspect," Sharon added, "is privacy. We each have separate quarters. No matter how much we care about each other, there are times we need to be alone."

"I can see where that would be especially true for married home sharers."

Lack of money in our economy has worked to bring people together. In our area I've seen two to three families, and sometimes more, merge their assets to invest in acreage.

Money shortage has also worked to bring families back together. A youngster who may have moved out at twenty, moves back home because he can't afford living on his own. This can be looked at in different ways. Older sons and daughters can be a blessing provided they can accept the responsibility of home sharing. Expect room-and-board payments if they are working and assistance with household chores.

In addition to the returning son or daughter, add Grandma or Grandpa. In many cases, our senior citizens can't live on their limited income.

These ideas of extended families may seem about as hard to digest as wallpaper paste. We've become a separated society. But larger family groups can be rewarding. I know. I grew up in the extended family situation. The big, white house in Barton, North Dakota, housed my grandma and grandpa, two aunts, one uncle, my mother, and me. It was a time of economic depression. My father had tuberculosis and lived in a sanitarium. We bonded together in hard times, but it's those times that evoke my most pleasant and warmest childhood memories.

With money again becoming tighter than the security around the president, maybe it's time to consider sharing. The concept of sharing the load is an old one. So old, in fact, it's written about in the Bible. The author of Ecclesiastes tells us, "Two are better than one because they have a good return for their labor. For if either of them falls, the one will lift up his companion . . . A cord of three strands is not quickly torn apart" (4:9, 10, 12 NASB).

We need each other. Get together and brainstorm ways to share.

If you're interested in saving money with a friend, maybe you'd be even more interested in making money with a friend. Skip along into part III and I'll share a gold mine of money-making ideas.

PART III
Money-Makers and How to Pad the Pot

Have you managed to wire the jaws of your money-eaters yet? Have you fine tuned your savings techniques? If not, don't despair. The only thing fast about making changes is the decision to change. The actual alterations in life-style can take years.

In this section I've included some "hot tips" you may want to include in your short- and long-range goals to help you pad your financial pot.

Hang on and we'll zip through ways you can earn extra income at home. With all these money-making schemes, you can beef up that scrawny budget without experiencing the Working Mother Guilts. Your children won't have to run an ad like this in the classifieds:

NEEDED: Stay-at-home MOM.
Must cook meals and bake cookies.
To apply call
060-8437.

In addition to covering homegrown income, we'll plunge headlong into investments and learn how our money makes money. Now don't let the word *investments* make you jittery. I promise to keep it simple. I will, too. Like Tilly, when the financial lingo rolls off the tongues of money changers, I feel about as intelligent as a chimpanzee in a class of anthropologists.

12
Income Extras From Your Time, Trash, Talent, and Treasures

THERE ARE AS MANY WAYS TO EARN EXTRA INCOME AT home as there are tadpoles in Burnt Bridge Creek. In this chapter we'll only skim the surface, but the samplings may stimulate you into starting a whole new career.

The first enterprising money-maker is sales. Now, I don't mean pavement-pounding, door-knocking kind of sales. I'm talking garage sales; attic, yard, auction, and estate sales; and flea markets.

While these exciting adventures won't bring immediate affluency, they certainly can help pad the pot.

"Dare to Dump It"

"But what can I sell? Where do I start?" If those are your questions, read on.

These days you can sell almost anything. To begin, take inventory. The best time for a garage sale is after spring cleaning. Go through every room, drawer, closet, and cupboard for items you no longer use. This is no time for nostalgia. Sure your fourteen-year-old's baby stroller brings back memories of the way he was, but he outgrew it twelve years ago. I used to think I would save all my kids' baby things for my grandchildren. When they got to their teens I'd look at all the infant paraphernalia and get blubbery. *My babies are growing up. Soon they'll have little ones of their own and I can get rid of this stuff.* With that thought I'd go into shock and pray the babies wouldn't come too soon. I finally sold everything at my garage sale.

If and when my grandchildren need these baby items, who knows, maybe I'll be able to find them at *your* garage sale.

As you are sorting through years of collected trash and treasures keep this theory in mind. In a book entitled *Sidetracked Home Executives,* Pam Jones and Peggy Young suggest that if you haven't "... cooked with it, danced with it, sat on it, squeezed into it, mailed it, read, or watered it in the last twelve months ..." you probably never will, so pitch it. Their motto is, "Dare to Dump It." Make it yours too.

As you explore your home for possible saleable items, keep in mind the more popular attractions to garage sale customers. Merchandise that sells well includes antiques, books, linens, kitchen items, children's toys and baby equipment, memorabilia, and bookcases.

Objets d'Art and Other Fine Saleables

Suppose in your house inventory you come across ten years' worth of art or craft projects you've created. Sell your talents for cash. While these fine art objects don't usually bring top dollar at garage sales, you can sell them at a profit in local art or craft shows, or your own home salesroom.

Arts and crafts, by the way, provide an excellent part-time job. Think of the possibilities. You can stay at home (except for occasional art shows and sales), enjoy your favorite hobby, and make money all at the same time.

Whatever you decide to sell, it may help you to know how to sell it.

How to Sell Almost Anything, Almost Anywhere

Some of you may be saying, "Sell? Me? Ha! My selling ability runs about as high as a subterranean mine shaft." You don't have to be a super salesperson to set up a garage sale, or any other kind of sale. What you do need is the right mind-set. Your decision to sell your trash or treasures instantly turns you into a saleswoman, a promoter, and a retailer. You are a professional businesswoman. As a businesswoman you'll want to gain the most return for your efforts.

Having attended and arranged numerous art shows, as well as garage sales, I'd like to share a few helpful tips that can make your sale a success.

A Garage Sale by Any Other Name . . .

Once you've put on your businesswoman's hat, you'll want to get on with business. And, one of the first steps in arranging a sale is deciding what to call it and where to hold it.

Suit the title and location to the type of merchandise you will be selling. For example, if Aunt Bertha left you an attic full of antiques, you'll probably want to label your business venture an Antique Sale, or Estate Sale. On the other hand, if most of your collection fits more comfortably into the used, slightly used, or junk area, you'll draw more of the buying customers if you call it a Garage Sale, an Attic Sale, a Yard Sale, or a Rummage Sale.

The title lets people know what to expect. Your location depends on the quality of your wares and what you decide to call it. Garages, for instance, are great places for garage sales. But if you're selling heirlooms, arts, crafts, or antiques, you'll probably want to locate in a family room or patio. The higher the quality, the classier the salesroom. Choose your title and location to complement your merchandise.

Clean Up Your Act

Whatever the caliber of your merchandise, you'll want it and your sales area clean and presentable. That includes your garage or attic. Items that won't be for sale should be transferred into a locked or closed off storage area. Visit several sales similar to the one you'll be having. Note the overall appearance, display areas you especially like, and prices. A little presale detective work can give you confidence for setting up your own sale. If you have the time, clean, wash, or dust your for-sale items. You'll be able to demand a slightly higher price if your wares sparkle. Of course, this isn't a priority, but personally, I like the uncluttered look.

Along with cleanup come the layout and design. At this point I imagine some of you are groaning, "Good grief, it's just a garage sale. I'm not expecting a visit from the First Lady."

That's true. However, neatly arranged tables to display your wares give the customers a better view. Simply set up your display in the way you'd like to see other people's sales. I've been to some sales where I stumbled through a stash of empty cans and bottles, tripped over a lawnmower, and wandered through a maze of a to-be-rebuilt engine in order to examine a bookcase.

While you don't want to turn your garage into a retail showroom, you will want to provide a clutter-free floor, tidy displays, and generous aisles for your customers.

Promotion

The key to success in your sales business is promotion. Advertise. Start early by painting large, attractive signs to place on main thoroughfares near your home. You'll need at least three. One of those should be placed near your driveway. Set your signs out about two hours before the sale is due to begin. Test drive past the signs and your home. Are the signs readable and clear? Some of the signs I've seen lately have been hard to read at two feet. Remember, your reader will probably be deciphering your message from thirty feet away, while traveling at twenty-five to thirty-five miles per hour.

I've used two-by-three-foot plywood boards, a quarter of an inch thick for my signs. I whitewash them and neatly paint my ad in large, black lettering. Oh yes, when you place your signs around the neighborhood, don't use the PUD poles (telephone or utility poles). It's against the law.

My friend Lauraine answered her door one day and a great, gruff, burly lineman towered in the doorway.

"This yours?" he growled, holding her cardboard sign in his massive fist.

"Ah—da—yes," Lauraine smiled meekly.

"It's illegal to tack up signs on the poles. The nail holes invite termites and eventually rot the wood. I could fine you, but this time I'll just give you a warning. Don't do it again."

"Y—yes—s sir." Lauraine's voice quivered. "Lesson learned."

So, if you don't want to tangle with a modern version of Paul Bunyan, avoid the poles. Instead use a freestanding, plywood sign, two pieces of wood attached at the top by hinges.

In addition to the signs, run a classified ad. Consider running the ad the day before the sale and the day of the sale. Your ad should include:

1. The type of sale—yard, garage, attic, antique, art, and so on.

2. The day, date, hours, address, and special items of interest that you think might draw customers.

Your ad should look something like this:

ESTATE SALE—Fri. & Sat., June 4–5, 8–4PM, 315 Saratoga, Lakewood, claw-foot tub, hide-a-bed, baby furniture.

When you run an ad, let the customer know what to expect. My artsy friends and I had a sale a few months ago. Our advertising told potential clients exactly what we had to offer. Our art sale included pottery, calligraphy, and drawings. In addition to our ad, we made up flyers that gave more detailed information. Our calligrapher did the honors and produced the masterpiece on page 112. Create your own flyer using your unique ideas to advertise that special sale.

Sales Go Better With Friends

Five of us artists got together to put on the art sale I told you about. By joining forces we were able to split advertising costs and time. Together we had more variety and a greater selection of artwork.

My last garage sale came about through the efforts of a neighbor, my mother, mother-in-law, and sister-in-law. It not only saves money and time, a joint venture also gives you someone to talk to if nobody shows up at your sale.

When the Price Is Right

Earlier, when I wrote about cleaning up your salesroom, I mentioned visiting other sales and checking out prices. This aspect is very important, because if your prices are too high your profit will be low. As you tour the sales in your neighborhood, compare your merchandise with theirs and price accordingly.

Take the time to mark the prices on your wares. I use those half-inch, round, self-adhesive stickers. Of course, you won't have to label everything. Your twenty men's ties could go in a box with a large label: Ties/50¢ each, or Make Offer. A professional pricing system tells people you care about the merchandise as well as their eyesight and comfort.

An occasional home-type sale may not stuff your pocketbook, but it helps to pad the pot. And better yet, the thought

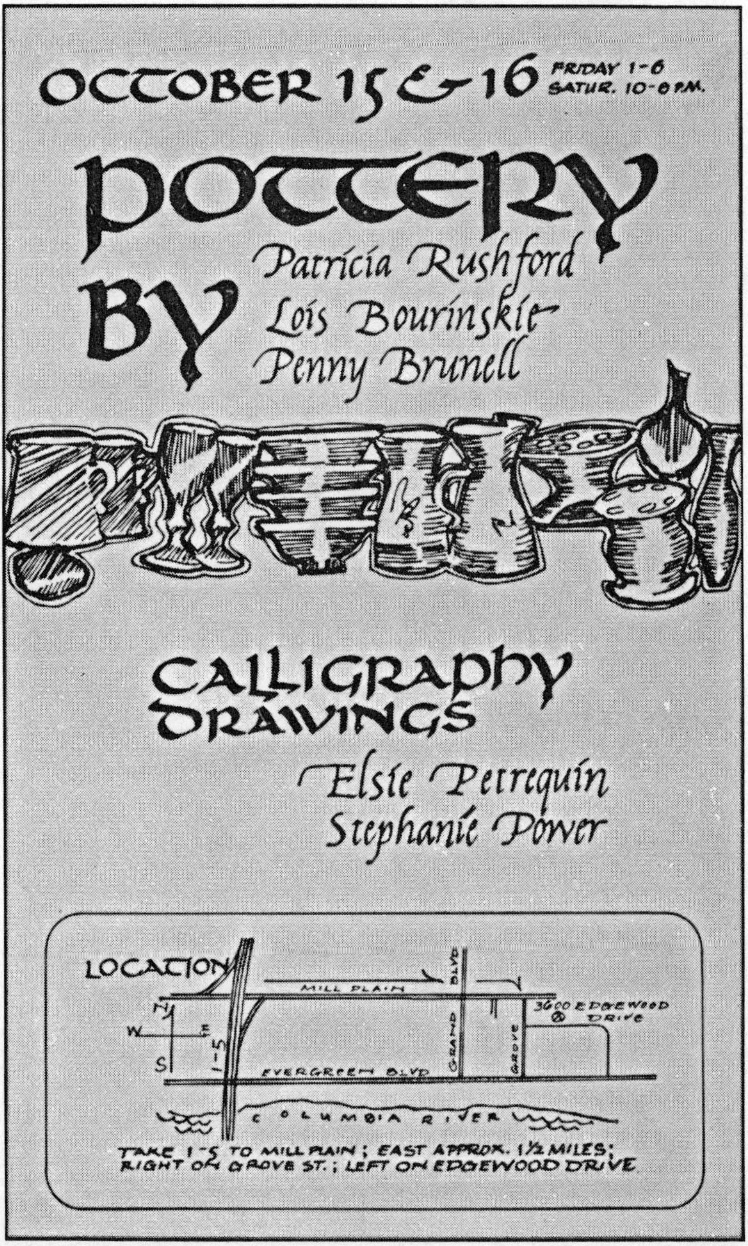
OCTOBER 15 & 16
FRIDAY 1-6
SATUR. 10-6 P.M.
POTTERY
BY
Patricia Rushford
Lois Bourinskie
Penny Brunell
CALLIGRAPHY
DRAWINGS
Elsie Petrequin
Stephanie Power
LOCATION
MILL PLAIN
GRAND BLVD
3600 EDGEWOOD DRIVE
N
W
E
S
I-5
EVERGREEN BLVD
GROVE
COLUMBIA RIVER
TAKE I-5 TO MILL PLAIN; EAST APPROX. 1½ MILES;
RIGHT ON GROVE ST.; LEFT ON EDGEWOOD DRIVE

of extra cash gives me the incentive to clear my home of excess inventory. Besides sales, there are dozens of other ways to earn extra money without having your family file your name under missing persons.

Career Ideas for You

If you're beginning to feel ambitious about bringing in some extra cash and remaining at home, you'll love the rest of this chapter. No matter what age you are, or what you do, if you're looking for money-makers, you're on the right page.

You'll notice I said any age. Are you still active at sixty-five and eager to earn your way? Be a grandma for a day—with pay. In other words, baby-sit, or house-sit. Pet-sit?

Whatever your age, you're too young to retire. Offer services for hire. Do you like to sew? My friend Marie works at home as a seamstress. Besides sewing clothes for half the town of Battle Ground, she mends clothes and does alterations. She also sews costumes for a costume shop. Marie even made an evening dress for one of our Miss Washingtons.

What do you do best? Tennis? Writing? Pottery? Weaving? Singing? Turn your hobby or area of expertise into a profitable business venture by offering classes in your home, or selling your creations.

Do you have an aptitude for math, a foreign language, or English? Provide help to the weary as a tutor. To spark your imagination, I've concocted a chart. On the left, locate your special gift or interest. The column on the right tells you how to turn talent into treasure.

Things I do best	How to make money at it
Talk on the telephone	Telephone sales; answering service.
Cook/Serve	Catering service; package and sell specialty foods such as cookies, bread, and so on.

Things I do best	How to make money at it
Work with numbers	Bookkeeping/Accounting; offer to balance Tilly's checkbook.
Type	Typing service: manuscripts, themes, term papers.
Sing	Give lessons; sing at weddings, funerals, anniversaries; deliver singing telegrams dressed as a chicken.
Grow things (plants, not babies)	Hang a shingle: "Plant Doctor"; winter-over plants in your greenhouse; grow & sell herbs or grow & sell anything.
Calligraphy (other art)	Sell it; teach it.
Photography	Photo journalism; set up a studio and offer passport pictures, portraits, weddings, and special occasions.
Interior Decorating	Use your home as a model then advertise your talents.
Needlework	Create and sell your embroidery (a lost art?); teach knitting, crocheting, needlepoint, tapestry, or quilting.
Write	Be a newspaper stringer. Write a how-to book; free-lance, copy edit, proofread, or index. (Danger: this occupation could be habit forming.)
Read	Be a proofreader or book reviewer.
Sales	In addition to garage sales and so on, be a sales representative part-time; got a great idea people can't live without? Sell it by mail. (Check U.S. postal regulations first.)

Have I primed your creative pump and gotten the imagination flowing? With that imagination and your special gift, you can be your own boss and build a small business. Be careful though, I know of too many women whose "mini" jobs turned into mega corporations.

As you forge ahead into that land of making money, keep one very important goal in mind. Set your sights not on the treasures the job could bring, but on doing God's will. I believe God would like us all to be productive in serving Him. So, before you start, pray and ask according to God's will. He will hear you. (1 John 5:14.)

Whether your business profits or loses, you'll want to slip on over to chapter 13 where we'll take a look at how to watch your money make money in the land of investments.

13

Make Your Money Make Money

SO FAR, WE'VE LEARNED HOW TO STARVE THE MONEY-eaters, use our time and talents to save money, and earn extra income. If we follow all this advice, we should have leftover money at the end of the month. Thus comes the question, *What do I do with all my savings?*

The answer is simple, invest it. Perhaps you are frowning and thinking, *I've saved and earned and I still run short of money, there's nothing left to invest.*

Invest? Me?

Remember the story in the Bible where the master got heavy-handed with the steward who buried his portion of wealth? " 'You wicked and slothful servant . . .' " the master said to him, " '. . . you ought to have invested my money with the bankers, and at my coming I should have received what was my own with interest' " (Matthew 25:26, 27 RSV).

This parable tells me two important things about money.

First, all that we have is given to us as a trust from God, and second, we are to be wise investors and stewards.

This doesn't mean we are to grab up a month's salary and blow the bundle on "pork belly futures." That could be as ridiculous as buying a thousand pounds of ice and storing it in the sun. While some financial planners encourage us to be "bullish" in our investments, the Bible takes a different view.

The wise King Solomon tells us, "Steady plodding brings prosperity; hasty speculation brings poverty" (Proverbs 21:5 TLB).

Take time to learn about the various investment programs before you take the plunge. While you are learning investment strategies, set goals. You can start your plans now.

Open a Savings Account

Every financial planner or adviser I have talked with insists that your first plan of investment should be to put a certain amount from each paycheck into a savings account. Most of these experts suggest that you accumulate three to six months' worth of income (minus taxes) in a secure and liquid account in case of emergencies.

Liquid, of course, meaning easy to get to. And, yes, it is a lot of money, let's say from six to ten thousand.

"Yipes," my friend Sharon gasped. "That would take me ten years."

"Don't let the amount intimidate you," I smiled. "The idea here is to start a savings account now. You only have a dollar a week extra? Save it. Once you get into the habit of saving, you can set higher goals."

"In other words," Sharon sighed, "develop discipline. Discipline yourself to diet, discipline to get housework done, discipline to save money. . . . Will it ever end?"

"Probably not. Don't forget who you're talking to. It's me, remember? The gal who started with such a long list of undeveloped disciplines I could have filled a phone book. We just have to work at them—one at a time. You want to be a better money manager don't you? And this is one discipline you should work on right away."

"Is saving money all that important?" Sharon mused. "Some of my Christian friends have told me that if I save up money I'm not trusting God to provide for my needs. You know that Bible verse in Matthew where Jesus says not to lay up treasures and not to worry about our clothes and food? I'm supposed to trust God for my needs. How can I show faith in God to care for all my needs if they are all met through my saved money?"

Sharon's question isn't an unusual one. I've stumbled over that verse myself. But, after some praying and Bible study, I've come to a conclusion. Of course God provides for my needs. However, he has also provided me with brains and an able body. I think God expects me to work and earn my own way as soon as I'm able. As 2 Thessalonians 3:10, 12 (RSV) says, ". . . If any one will not work, let him not eat." Idle busybodies are to ". . . do their work in quietness and to earn their own living." I see the ability to provide for future and present needs as a gift from God.

Remember Joseph and what he did when he learned of a predicted famine? He saved from what was harvested during the prosperous years. What he had saved kept them alive during those seven years of famine. He could have insisted, "The Lord will provide," but instead Joseph used his head. The Lord had provided him with wisdom to meet the problem and expected Joseph to use his good sense to find a solution. He did.

Actually, we're commanded to store and provide for more difficult times. Check out the ant in Proverbs 6:6–11, and the prudent son in Proverbs 10:5. Then take a look at 1 Timothy 5:8, "If any one does not provide for his relatives, and especially for his own family, he has disowned the faith and is worse than an unbeliever" (RSV).

There you have it. I rest my case. We are to provide for

emergencies. The best time to begin storage preparation is now. As I told Sharon, the amount you save doesn't have to be big enough to buy the bank. Just save something—*anything.* Were you able to put your money-eaters on a fasting program? Have you spent less using some of the ideas in part II? Can you earn extra income from brainstorming in chapter 14? Great, then open a passbook savings account.

Congratulations! You Are Now an Investor.

Yes, opening a passbook savings account ushers you over the border, into the Land of Investments. Now, whatever you do, don't get all excited and brag to all your financial-genius friends that you've just invested in "passbook savings." They'll think you crossed the border into hysteria instead of investments. Passbook accounts are as unpopular to financial experts as booking passage on the Titanic.

Why? Because 5¼ percent interest, when you deduct inflation and taxes, will leave you with less real buying power than you had to begin with. "But," you may be stammering, "if I'm losing money why bother?"

Because, it earns more than storing your loot underground. The idea behind a passbook account is to start the saving habit and accumulate enough cash to invest in more lucrative money-makers. "Enough" cash means around $1,000.

Exploring the Land of Investments

If you still find saving money harder than Superman's chest, consider an automatic monthly withdrawal from your checking account to your savings account. Or, if you or your spouse work where a credit union is available, arrange for a payroll deduction. These methods are usually painless and not subject to whether or not you get around to it.

Once you've tucked away $1,000, you're ready to transfer your savings to a higher-yield instrument.

"A what?" If you've just heaved an exasperated and confused sigh and asked that question, relax. You don't have to resign yourself to the bottom end of the financial genius scale because you don't understand the language.

I must admit, however, some of the lingo in the Land of Investments made me feel as significant as a fruit fly in a herd of elephants. It used to overwhelm me. Consequently, one of the first strategies for surviving in the financial jungle is to learn the language.

As a first lesson, let's go back to the phrase I used a couple paragraphs ago—*higher-yield instrument.* Did it throw you? Higher yield simply means earning a higher interest rate, or getting more for your money. The various savings plans, or types of investment, are often referred to as vehicles or instruments.

As you explore this unpredictable land, you'll undoubtedly stumble over the Money Market Mainland, muddle through the Mutual Fund Maze, and stagger through the Stock Market. Knowing a little about these investment vehicles can make your journey safer and more interesting.

What is a money market? Perhaps the question has been burning in your brain for years. Or, maybe it only rates second in priority to, "How can I get the gum off my kid's eyelashes?" Whether you want it or not, here is the answer. A money market is a transaction in which money is bought, sold, or traded. When businesses or institutions want to borrow large sums of money on a short-term basis (less than a year), they often call the investment a money market.

Say for example, the First National Bank of No Deposit No Return wants to borrow $10,000. You have the cash and the bank lures you with an interest rate you can't refuse. You receive an IOU with a promise that they will return all your money plus interest at the end of a specified time period.

Why does the bank need to borrow money? So they can loan it out at a higher interest rate than they are paying you, so they can earn enough money to make ends meet.

You can get into some money markets for around $1,000. As I indicated, they are usually short-term investments, maturing in less than a year, they offer high safety and high liquidity—that is, they're easy to get at.

Money markets include such instruments as Treasury Notes and Bills, which are obligations of the U.S. government making them comparatively risk free. Because these government issues offer security, they tend to yield less than other instruments. Other money market labels include certificates of deposit, commercial paper, and banker's acceptances.

I mention money markets here, not because I feel they are always a great investment, but because they are a likely second step after the passbook savings account. Other instruments to consider at this point are saving certificates, savings bonds, U.S. Treasury Bills, and money market mutual funds. Whichever vehicle you choose during this first part of your journey into the land of making money, look for investments that give you high interest, high liquidity, and high safety.

Speaking of "highs," you'll notice that one of the major attractions in the Land of Investments is the mutual fund maze. I call it a maze because mutual funds offer more investment avenues than there are quills on a porcupine. Beginning investors find mutual funds advantageous for several reasons. First, diversification. Financial counselors implore their clients to diversify. What does it mean? Why? Quite simply, this principle follows the old saying, "Don't put all your eggs in one basket." If all your savings are tied up in a single investment and the bottom falls out, all you end up with is an empty basket, or nest, or pocketbook.

Diversify! Diversify everything, including your checking and savings. Banks and other financial institutions occasionally bottom out. We can't afford to entrust all of our assets in what has always been considered a secure and insured risk. Individual commercial bank savings accounts are protected under the FDIC (Federal Deposit Insurance Corporation) for up to $100,000. Savings and Loans carry the same $100,000 protection through FSLIC (Federal Savings and Loan Insurance Corporation). However, as Venita VanCaspel says, in her book *The Power of Money Dynamics,* "if there should be a run on the banks, the $100,000 would be hard to deliver. If that should occur, only about 2 percent of all bank deposits could probably be paid off under the guarantee."

Mutual funds provide diversification. Some of the different avenues in which mutual funds invest are stocks, bonds, real estate, and money markets. Also, mutual funds introduce the novice investor into the Land of Investments through the use of a qualified tour guide, otherwise known as a financial planner. Note: Financial planners are stockbrokers, but not all stockbrokers are financial planners.

This individual's experience and training helps new explorers to learn survival techniques and the language. The qualified financial planner can offer you an active part in the investment game at a reduced risk.

Third, mutual funds offer the convenience of constant supervision. Once you and your financial planner have selected the fund or funds relative to your needs, you can leave your investment in the planner's capable hands and pursue other interests. Do, however, follow your investments and check on your planner and your progress on a regular basis.

Fourth, mutual funds allow you to invest with as little as $100—some even less. Low investments like these are possible because mutual funds are based on pooling money from several investors into one fund. This fund is managed by professional managers.

While there are many advantages to mutual funds, approach the mutual fund maze as you would investigate the anatomy of a porcupine—very carefully. Some mutual funds can be as safe as a baby kangaroo in his mother's pouch. Other funds are riskier than setting sail in a leaky tub. Not every mutual funds manager or program can be trusted. Baby kangaroos have been known to fall out of their pouches. But, consider mutual funds. Find a financial planner you can trust and go with the best-managed program.

Whether you choose the aid of an adviser or elect the do-it-yourself approach, take time to explore the land before you settle down.

As we journey deeper into the interior of the Land of Investments, we encounter the stock market. The stock market can be as appealing to the adventurous new investor as Las Vegas casinos are to a gambler.

As you hear the tales of million-dollar winners, your eyes may glow with dollar signs and your ears ring with the sound of silver. While you tune in the winners, listen also to the wails of the losers. According to a financial-adviser friend, nine out of ten people lose money playing the stock market. It's as much a gamble as lottery tickets, roulette, blackjack, and the one-armed bandits.

Before you play the market, learn the rules of the game. Don't invest unless you are prepared to risk the loss. The problem with most investors in the market, I'm told by the experts, is that they panic when their stock or stocks drop. They wrongly buy when the stock is up and sell when the price goes down. Ideally, the game is played most profitably when stock is purchased during a "bear" market and sold in a "bull" market.

At this point you may be asking, "Are we talking about stocks or livestock?" If that's your question, let's stop for another brief language lesson. A *bear market* means buying is down and things are not going so well at the stock exchange. I suppose they call it *bear* because everyone is so grumpy. A *bull market* means sales are up and investors are feeling as cocky as a bull during the mating season.

Until you are well educated in the ups and downs and bears and bulls of the stock market, enter with caution. The "bullpen" and the "bear's den" are as dangerous to amateurs as a lion to a lame gazelle.

Me? I prefer to be escorted through the market, advised by a trusted and competent financial adviser.

I'll be sharing some pointers on how to choose a financial counselor in the next few pages, but first, I want to introduce you to an investment you can't afford to ignore.

As you tour the Land of Investments you're certain to find shelter in I.R.A. and Keogh. These are the two most friendly terms in this land. They offer a way to reduce taxes and prepare for your golden autumn, otherwise known as retirement.

The I.R.A. (not to be confused with ERA) is short for Individual Retirement Account. At last, a tax shelter we can all take advantage of. It's called a tax shelter because an I.R.A. protects a certain amount of money each year from the money-eating jaws of the Infernal Revenue Service.

How does it work? You are permitted to invest up to $2,000 per year of your taxable income and you don't pay taxes on it until it is withdrawn at retirement. An additional $250 can be put into an I.R.A. account for a nonworking spouse. If both husband and wife are working, each is entitled to invest $2,000.

The I.R.A. monies must be taken out of earned income, not interest income. And, there are penalties for early withdrawal so you'll be encouraged to leave your nest egg alone until you really need it. Withdrawal can begin when you are fifty-nine and a half years of age. If you withdraw your money early, you must pay the deferred taxes plus a 10 percent penalty.

A Keogh account is also a retirement fund and tax-deferred savings account. But this one is set up for the self-employed individual. If you have your own business, you can, at this writing, qualify for both plans. A self-employed person can invest 15 percent of his or her income into a Keogh account. Again, there is a penalty for early withdrawal.

Because these accounts are subject to change by the U.S. government, check with an IRS agent or tax accountant before you set up the account or fill out your tax forms.

I strongly urge you to set up an I.R.A. or Keogh account. Start saving now. The sooner you begin, the fluffier your cushion will be when you retire. Let's face it, old bones rest easier when the feathers are deeper.

Where will the money come from? With all the money you'll save with the helpful hints offered in this book, you should have your nest egg well under construction within a year. The squeeze you may feel in saving money during your income-producing years will be like a cuddle compared to the crushing reality of a lost job and no visible means of support, or retirement with only Social Security which is no security at all.

Once you've set up your I.R.A. and/or Keogh account, you will want to invest it. As you can see, there are as many ways to invest your money as there are needles on a pine tree. Be especially careful with these accounts. Look for low-risk investments that offer you highest yields.

You've wandered around and gotten a tourist's view of the Land of Investments. Maybe you accumulated a sizeable savings account and muddled through the maze of mutual funds and crossed the money market mainland prosperously. Perhaps you outran the bear, rode the bull, and swept through the stock market unscathed. Or, maybe you bypassed the market entirely. Whatever your situation, you like the lay of the land and want a piece of the real estate action.

Should you invest in real estate? Certainly—if . . .

- if you've taken enough time to understand and research the various types of properties available and methods of investing.
- if you have the ability to accurately assess the value of a given property.
- if you know an expert real estate broker or investor you can trust to advise you as you learn about this very complex area of investing.

You can invest in real estate without the hassle of doing it all yourself, however, through limited partnerships. This avenue is fast becoming as popular among novice investors as mutual funds because both offer such a wide variety of investment opportunities. In addition to real estate, with limited partnerships you can buy into gas and oil, cable television, equipment leasing, and the list goes on and on. You'll want to check with your financial planner or broker for more information before you stroll down this fascinating lane.

It seems that nearly every turn on the road through the Land of Investments requires special skills and experience to smoothly execute the curves, avoid drop-offs and washouts, and set a straight and narrow course toward financial security.

I've also indicated time and again the importance of wise and trusted financial counselors. These experienced persons can map your course and help you investigate the many roads to riches—or rags. You may think you don't need guides. But, should you choose to travel alone, learn before you leap. The less thought you put into any investment, the more likely you are to lose the money. Just as a surgeon's mind is filled with every detail of the human anatomy before surgery, the investor must know the anatomy of investments. The same rules apply—know what you are doing before you take the first step.

Since I am not an expert financial investor, I prefer to let my tour guide steer me onto the paths of richest returns.

"So," you may ask, "how do I find this most trusted and expert counselor?"

Proverbs 15:22 tells us, "Without counsel plans go wrong, but with many advisers they succeed" (RSV). This verse indicates that I should get my advice from several sources. And that, even if I decide on the do-it-yourself course, some advice from others is wise.

Here are some things you need to know about financial

counselors, advisers, and so on, and tips for choosing the right one for you.

Financial planners can help you with all your money concerns, investments as well as budgeting and getting your spending under control. They cost money. Some require an up-front fee, while others make their living on commissions from their clients' investment earnings. Not all brokers or financial planners can be trusted. Not all brokerages (businesses through which you invest in mutual funds or stocks) are reputable. Take care in choosing both the firm and the adviser, or you may wake up to find the business and your money disappearing on the "fly-by-night express."

Here are some tips to help you find a counselor who will serve you well.

1. Choose a reputable firm. A nationally known brokerage, such as E. F. Hutton or Merrill Lynch, will want to maintain a high quality of service to their clients. A novice investor has the potential to become an influential client who can bring them high commissions. Check your phone book for financial planners, counselors, and brokers. Ask your investor friends for their recommendations.

2. When you find a firm, talk with the manager. Explain your financial needs. In that explanation include how much you want to invest and what investment areas interest you. You see, even choosing a counselor is an art, and you need a working knowledge of the investment game. Tell the manager you want an agent or adviser who can communicate the complications of finances in easy-to-understand language.

3. Once you find a recommended adviser, set up a half-hour consultation appointment. Most professionals will offer a "get acquainted" meeting free, or for a reduced fee. This is your chance to interview as well as be interviewed. Feel free to ask questions such as:

- How long have you worked as a financial adviser?
- Are you a certified financial planner?

- What is your area of expertise? (An expert in the stock market may walk you into a dead end in mutual funds.)
- How much do you charge? (Many brokers make commission only, while others charge a flat fee and/or commission. Know before you go.)

While you talk, check out your prospective tour guide for compatibility. Does his or her financial lingo leave you feeling as though your brains have been remodeled? Are your questions being answered, sidestepped, or ignored? Agents who talk over your head and try to impress you are often inexperienced. The wiser and more experienced broker will adjust explanations to your level of understanding. Even if you understand each other, you may not be able to work together. Try to pinpoint your comfort zone. Does the adviser seem to fit like your favorite slippers? Or, do you feel like your slip is showing, your mascara is smudged, and your nylons have runs? Go for the slippers.

4. It's easier, of course, to spend or risk other people's money than it is your own. By the way, it's fair to ask an adviser if he/she owns or has invested in whatever they offer you. Once you've chosen a counselor, make your goals clear. Regardless of the guide's abilities, keep a watchful eye on your investments.

No matter how much care you take to choose the right financial planner for you, you still risk the possibility of making a wrong choice. Just as in any investment you make, there is always the possibility of failure. There are no "sure investments," only risks. For this reason, we are told by Jesus not to depend on money or laid up treasures which rust, or become lost or stolen. Only heavenly treasures can be counted "secure." So let's conclude our travels in the Land of Investments, where money makes money—or loses it. It's time to move up the coast into budgets and records.

Don't look so sad. The fun isn't over. Join me in this next section, called "Paper-Weight Blues." The song may be bluesy, but we'll have some laughs while I help you build a budget and get your family involved. If your family is anything like mine, family-affair budgeting could be hilarious.

Then, I promise you a bit of fun as we climb the steps to organized money management through records in chapter 16 called, "Records, Taxes, and Tears."

Besides, if the Land of Investments left visions of dollar signs dancing in your head, you'll want to read on and learn how to budget those visions into reality by keeping records of all you earn.

PART IV
Paper-Weight Blues

I wish I could tell you that you can successfully deter the money-eaters, enjoy those money-saving ploys, and make lots of extra money without making plans or keeping records, but I can't. Along with the fun, comes work. But, I'm sure you won't mind, if in the process you evolve into a better money manager.

Work, like medicine, goes better with sugar. So let's see if we can't sweeten up the budgeting and record-keeping business with a "Bit-o-Humor" and put this job in its place—behind us.

Once we've tackled the paperwork, we'll embark on a special journey. This is an adventure you won't want to miss. Our voyage will take us up the golden steps to Financial Freedom.

In the meantime, grab your pencils and we'll sing, laugh, and dance our way through the Paper-Weight Blues.

14
Balancing Your Act

OUR FIRST SONG-AND-DANCE ROUTINE IS CALLED THE Budget Shuffle. I tried to shuffle it out the door, but to no avail. I searched for days to find an authority on finances who would say, "Budgets are for fanatics."

Instead, I found every expert, every book, and every seminar, stressed the importance of a working budget. "You can't manage your money without a budget," some would say. Others went so far as to tell me, "The chief cause of financial failure is the lack of proper budgeting."

What Is a Budget?

Many of these same experts who pointed out the importance of budgeting also concurred that budgets were ho-hum, boring, and no fun at all. Some people, when faced with a budget, turn pale and shake at the knees. The thought of confinement makes them break into a cold sweat. "It's too restrictive," Elizabeth squirms, "I don't like being controlled by a bunch of numbers."

Another free spender, Alice, describes a budget as a store where you buy all the things you don't need at a discount.

So far budgeting sounds as thrilling as operating a stopwatch at a snail race. But, before you let the thought of budgeting give you hives, let's find out what a budget really is.

A quick check with Webster's assured me that budgets were not the nose-wrinkling, yawn-producing task I imagined them to be. Quite simply, *budget* means to plan. Further, it is, "an estimate of future financial income and outgo."

Hmmm, a plan, or maybe you could even call it a goal. No one said it had to be elaborate. In fact, most of the books I've read stress the importance of it, then slyly change the subject. I've come to the conclusion that the keeping of a budget varies greatly from one individual to another. While some need minor guidelines, others require boundaries as heavily guarded as the Berlin Wall. In fact, my friend Penny falls into the "minor" league. "I never write out a budget. I don't need to," Penny claims. "I know exactly how much I bring in and pay out each month. My budget has been the same for years."

For Prudent Penny, the mind-over-money philosophy works fine, mostly because she plans ahead and never overspends.

However, if you handle money like rain, where it's either absorbed or it goes down the drain, you need a more structured method. Without limitations, you could spend yourself down the river into an ocean of debts.

Who Needs a Budget? or *How Do You Like "Designer Jeans Au Gratin?"*

It's obvious that everyone (especially self-disciplined people like Penny) doesn't need a formal budget. But everyone needs a plan to help her live within her means.

All businesses, in order to succeed, work within a budget. Even the government . . . well . . . let's just say they have one.

A young couple recently discovered the importance of budgeting. Their teacher? Experience. Nancy and Jim had enjoyed four short months of honeymoon when Jim flew out of town on a business trip. During his two-week absence, Nancy received both their paychecks and instructions from Jim to pay the bills. Since the banks had closed, Nancy cashed the checks at a local supermarket. "I'll deposit the money that's left tomorrow," she reasoned.

While Jim businessed in Ohio, neglected Nancy *managed* the money. She *managed* to sidestep the bank deposit, forget the bills, and spend the whole bundle. In addition, Nancy *managed* to run up over $5,000 on her Bank Americard.

By the time Jim returned, Nancy didn't even have enough money left to buy ingredients for dinner. She greeted her travel-weary husband at the door with, "Hi, Honey! How do you like Designer Jeans Au Gratin?"

As Nancy confessed her accidental spending spree, Jim turned red.

"How could you do this?" he raged. "It will take at least a year to pay off these debts. What did you buy?"

"Things," Nancy winced.

"Things! You spent $6,000 on *things?*"

"Well . . . I wanted to surprise you. I painted the bedroom and got new drapes and a chair. I found a great buy on a new sewing machine. And, you know I've been wanting a digital radio alarm. Sears had one on sale. Now we can wake up to music instead of that horrid buzz. Oh . . . and best of all," she finished proudly, "Sak's had a fabulous sale on my favorite designer jeans—only $40 a pair. I saved over $200 on four of them."

"That's great, Honey," Jim shook his head. "But if you keep saving money at this rate, we'll go bankrupt."

Nancy frowned and chewed her lower lip. "Jim, I'm sorry.

It's just . . . well . . . it was lonely without you. I didn't mean to spend the money—it—it sort of disappeared. Jim . . . ," she approached him cautiously, "we could borrow some money from Dad."

"No!" he snapped. "We'll handle it ourselves." Jim's voice softened as he spotted the dejected expression on his wife's face. "Look, Honey, it'll work out. Besides, I have an idea—we'll take it all back—except for the paint."

"Huh? Oh yeah! I hadn't thought of that. Oh . . . the jeans. I can't return them—final sale."

Jim pulled her gently into his arms and grinned. "That's okay, as long as I don't have to eat them."

"What?" Nancy frowned.

"The jeans. You asked me if I liked Designer Jeans Au Gratin. Actually, Jeans à la Nancy suits me better."

Nancy and Jim spent the rest of the evening forgiving and forgetting. They made plans for a new future, with an adjusted budget which, Jim advised, they would work on together.

Not every misappropriation of funds case can claim a happy ending. Some end up in divorce, bankruptcy, or even jail.

As I said earlier, a budget doesn't have to be time-consuming or elaborate. If you've never kept track of your spending before, however, your first few months could prove demanding. But, once the budget is set up, the time you spend on it is entirely up to you.

The success or failure of budgets depends largely on attitudes. Don't think of your budget as an imprisonment. You aren't confined within the walls of what a budget dictates. After all, you're the one who built those walls in the first place. You can tear them down or move them out. Think of your budget as a guideline you have chosen to set up. With it you know what you earn and spend. Your budget becomes a tool that helps you dispense your funds when and where you decide. Through a budget you can watch your savings grow and plan investments for the future. For those who now live in the frustrating bonds of mismanagement and overspending, it can mean financial freedom.

In order to maintain a budget and live within the goals you must think positive rather than negative. Think *goal*, not limit. Think *plan*, not prison. Think *yes*, not maybe.

One more thought I'd like to leave you with as to the "why budget" question is this: Our Lord expects us to plan ahead. In Luke 14:28, 29, Jesus says, "For which of you, desiring to build a tower, does not first sit down and count the cost, whether he has enough to complete it? Otherwise, when he has laid a foundation, and is not able to finish, all who see it begin to mock him" (RSV).

In other words it's foolish to start something you can't finish. If this principle applies to building a house, think how much more it should apply to our daily lives and our future.

Priority Budgeting

Now that we've established the importance of a budget, let's get on with the business of setting one up.

The first consideration when planning a budget is priorities—what's most important in your family. Each family will have developed an entirely different set of priorities, and as our families grow or change, so do the needs.

As your needs vary, so will your respective budgets. The only common ground we all have in establishing a budget is a limited income. We must live within that income boundary.

As we plan a budget, we would do well to think of money in terms of time. We are all accountable for a specific allotment of time. How we choose to spend that time directly affects the quality of our lives now and in the future. Spend both time and money wisely. Once spent—forever lost.

"Paradise Lost"—Budget Relocated

This phrase became startling reality to my friend Jennifer. Last year she lost not only considerable time and money, but tragically, her husband. A boating accident left her husband, Tom, in critical condition. After eight months of intensive care, he died.

Before the accident, Jennifer and Tom managed well on his $60,000-a-year income. Their priorities included a country estate, complete with horses, two new cars, a yacht, and four trips a year to "paradise." For Jennifer, paradise and a lot of other things were lost. Medical bills had eaten away at most of the family's liquid assets by the time Jennifer secured a job. Going from $60,000 a year to $10,800 was not going to be an easy adjustment. But, Jennifer smiled and said, "Guess we'll just have to tighten our belts and simplify."

Simplify she did. Have a look at Jennifer's simplified budget. (Figured on a monthly basis. See page 138.)

Even after Jennifer trimmed all the frills from the family's previous budget, she still had to cut even deeper to make ends meet.

"The hardest part about all this," Jennifer confesses, "is facing the bill collectors. I tell them I'll pay, if it takes me the rest of my life. Most of them are satisfied with that. They'd rather be paid a little than not at all. But some of them," she groaned, "make me feel like a criminal."

"You sound determined," I felt a little envious. "I wonder if I could be so brave."

"At first it seemed overwhelming. Then I sat down and wrote everything down—all our assets and liabilities. When it was all down on paper, I just started listing the things I could sell and narrowed the list down to what we really needed. Now," she sighed, "it looks like I'm down to selling my family in order to pay those medical bills."

My questioning look brought a twinkle to her eyes as she explained. "My horses, silly."

Item	Income	Expenses	Totals
Salary—after taxes	$ 648		$ 648
Total			$ 648
House payment—includes taxes		$ 325	
Second Mortgage		200	
House Insurance		25	
Car Insurance and License		25	
Loans: A—Roof repair		100	
B—Attorney fees ($4,500)		25	
C—Medical bills ($8,500)		50	
Child Care		55	
Groceries (for four)		240	
Utilities		100	
Telephone		30	
Medical/Dental		25	
Transportation (gas)		70	
Total Expenses		$1,270	−$1,270
Total over/short			($−622)

Jennifer has listed her home for sale and hopes to lower her budget and raise her salary to closer compatibility within the next year.

I used Jennifer as an example here, to show you that no matter how difficult your financial situation, you can be encouraged. By planning and setting goals on paper, or budgeting, you can see an end to many of the looming anxiety-producing money problems.

Jennifer has plotted out her budget and set some goals. Now it's your turn. The easiest way to start a project is to plunge in. So find yourself a worksheet and begin with me.

It's Your Turn

The first stage of budget plotting is to accumulate approximate figures for your income and expenses during the past few months to a year.

Maybe you're saying, "Whoa! How do I come up with these figures? I can't remember what I spent on groceries last week, let alone for the last month."

Good point. There's a simple solution, but you probably won't like it. Especially if you aren't too crazy about this "numbers racket" in the first place. Here's where developing a budget gives you an aerobic-style mental workout.

The most accurate method of determining your estimated expenses is to go back through your last year's checkbook and receipts. Record your findings on a worksheet. This initial budget is based on what you now spend—not on your future hopes. Under income, write down all expected income for the year and divide it by twelve to get the average income per month. Some of your monthly expenses will be fixed and easy to find. Others, like groceries and medical bills will be more difficult. Go back through the past year and total all medical and dental bills. Find the monthly average.

Now, if the thought of rummaging through a whole year's worth of bills just to come up with an estimate of one month's expenses has your blood pressure bounding, calm down. Not all of the expenses need to be based on a full year. Telephone, utilities, insurance payments, taxes, and licenses should be figured that way because they may not be paid each month, or may vary greatly from month to month.

As for groceries and clothing, you can venture a guess based on the previous three months. Of course, if the job still makes you feel like you are teetering on the edge of a cliff in a hurricane, you can come down from the dizzying heights and fake it. Make a wild guess, or base your budget on last month's expenses. However, you'll probably be making numerous adjustments on your guesses over the next few months until they fall close to your actual expenses.

Your final tallies should provide you with fairly accurate figures to place under the expense column of your monthly budget. Don't be surprised if the miscellaneous column scores high enough to win the title, "Misc. Money-Eater of the Year." Your budget, along with the information you gathered in chapter 2, should soon have her exposed figure under wraps.

Now we're ready to insert the estimated income and expense amounts on a budget worksheet. On this sample budget plan, mark those items that are pertinent to your family with a yellow marker. Then go back and fill in the blanks.

1. If you can't mark up the book, grab a pencil and label four columns as illustrated.

2. List all sources of expected income (If income varies, keep your guestimate low.)

ITEM	INCOME	EXPENSES	TOTAL
Income:			
Salary			
Salary—Spouse			
Real Estate income (rentals or contracts)			
Bonus/Commission			
Dividends/Interest income			
All other income			
Total Income			

Some of the experts I've read and talked with say you should include *all* income—interests, bonuses, dividends, and so on—in this budgeted income figure. I prefer, unless these represent a significant proportion of your income, that you forget them. Then, when the cash comes in, slip it smugly into your savings account. Blow it on a second honeymoon, or a trip to Guatemala, or a new dress. The possibilities are endless. It's always a thrill to receive an income that isn't already destined "bill-payer."

Oh, and please don't include money you expect to win

from the state lottery tickets, the Irish Sweepstakes, or Publisher's Clearinghouse. The income listed here should be more than a "sure thing."

Now that we've completed the easy and more enjoyable part of our budget, it's time to take a look at where our hard-earned money is spent.

ITEM	INCOME	EXPENSES	TOTAL
Fixed Expenses: Tithes (10% of gross or preference)			
Savings (try for 5% of net income)			
Mortgage/Rent			
Real Estate Taxes	(Often included in		
Home Insurance	Mortgage payment)		
Utilities (heat, electricity, water, garbage)			
Telephone			
Loans or Installments (car, boat, home improvement)			
Loan A			
Loan B			
Income Taxes			
Health & Life Insurance			
Union Dues			
Auto Insurance			
Other			
Total—Subtract from Income		$	−$
Total—left for variable expenses			$

3. List all fixed expenses. (These include obligations you must meet no matter what.) Round off figures to nearest ten. (See budget form on page 141.)

4. Subtract your total fixed expenses from your income. Hopefully you will have some money left over for the other necessities in life—such as food.

5. List all your variable expenses. (See page 143.) These are items you need or want. They are termed "variable" because the amounts may vary from month to month and because variables are the items that are most often cut or trimmed when the money runs out. The following list of variables may or may not be a part of your life-style. Again, feel free to use that yellow marker to underline the items you will use in your budget.

6. Subtract the variable expenses from the amount you have left over from paying the fixed expenses. This is the point in budgeting when you need someone beside you. This trusted friend will now assume one of two roles. One, she can help you celebrate—if you came out even or ended up with a profit. Two, she can pick you off the floor or hand you a box of Kleenex if you ended in the red.

So, how did you do? For those who came out on top, in the black, or pink, or whatever—congratulations! You are probably one of the few Americans who can claim success in living within their budgets. You have survived the deficit-spending bug. Deficit spending is catchy. Uncle Sam caught it years ago and has been spreading the disease around to citizens in epidemic proportions.

Unfortunately, while our great Uncle can get away with operating in the red, we can't. Spending money you don't have catches up with you and sends you into bankruptcy or behind bars.

"In the Pink"

"But I'm in the red and can't get out!" If that's your despairing cry, don't panic. There are solutions. Ask Jennifer.

ITEM	INCOME	EXPENSES	TOTAL
Variable Expenses: Groceries (Food and nonfood items, dining out)			
Household Maintenance			
Clothing			
Clothing Maintenance (Cleaning/Dry Cleaning)			
Home Furnishings and Equipment			
Transportation (car repairs, gas & oil, commuting)			
Medical/Dental			
Personal			
Child Care/Allowances			
Education			
Recreation			
Gifts/Christmas			
Recreation/Vacation			
Miscellaneous			
Total—Subtract from $ left for variable expense		$	−$
Total—over/short			$

Grab your pencil and start trimming. Slice off dollars on those items that mean the least to you.

We've already talked about ways of saving money on food, clothing, and household items. Start from the bottom of the expense list and work up. One good thing about red is that it can be diluted down to pink. And, "in the pink," as I understand it, is a bright and cheery place to be.

To make you even more cheery, how about a simplified budget. Sound good? While some of the more complex moneymaking and money-spending families will need a longer list of income and expense items, most of us can easily slip into this condensed version. (See page 145.)

Why Budgets Fail

Once you have cut your expenses and balanced them with your income, or come out with less expenses than income, your budgeting plan has succeeded. Now all you have to do is keep it up.

One of the main principles to remember in budgeting is that if you overspend in one area, you must compensate by underspending in another.

The biggest mistake new budgeters make is to use their savings as compensation for overspending. The savings account is a must and serves as a cushion or buffer in emergencies. A dwindled savings account could mean disaster if you suffer loss of income through job layoff, illness, accident, or death.

Monthly payments into a savings account can relieve the pressure of such an emergency. Most financial experts agree that our savings cushion should come to or exceed three months' wages. They also tell me it should be kept liquid.

You'll remember from my earlier remarks that liquid means "ready cash." Your liquid assets include checking accounts, passbook savings accounts, some money markets, mutual funds, mattresses, cookie jars, and broken sugar bowls.

No matter how desperate you are in your budget cuts, keep that eraser away from savings. While a vacation in a local campground may not seem as exciting as sunbaked Tahiti, at least when you come home you'll still have a cushion to fall back on.

INCOME	
Salary—Gross	$16,000
Interest/Dividends	1,200
Other Income	7,500
Total Income	$24,700
EXPENSES	
Tithes/Contributions	$ 2,500
Taxes	4,000
Savings	1,200
Rent/Mortgage	4,500
Food	3,000
Clothing	900
Medical/Dental	1,000
Insurance	450
Transportation	1,200
Utilities/Telephone	850
Personal	600
Entertainment/Vacation	1,000
Education	500
Household Purchases	400
Miscellaneous	350
Other	
Other	
Total Expenses	$22,450
Balance	$2,250

Besides flattening the savings cushion, other reasons for budget failure are:

1. Family members who don't understand budgeting or won't cooperate, better known as the keeping-up-with-the-Jones' ploy. Also referred to as *selfishness.*

2. Overspending, or the credit-card crazies.

3. Impulse buying and failure to use your talents to beat back inflation.

4. Trying to stretch your income to fit expenses rather than shrinking the expenses to slip easily into your income bracket. Or, more simply, failure to live within one's means.

It's not always easy to cut back on expenses. Sometimes you need to take a serious look at your priorities in life. If you are consistently living beyond your means, you may want to consider getting help from a Consumer Credit Counseling Service. This type of assistance is available throughout the United States. For information check with a local library or your phone book.

Whether or not you need counseling, stay tuned. You won't want to miss these next two chapters as we cover ways to avoid budget pitfalls. We'll also discover more useful hints to help you get back on your bucking budget and ride it into submission. This is no time to weaken and fall off. Sit tall. Grab the reins and repeat to yourself, *I'm in control.*

15

Budgeting-A Family Affair

BUDGETING—UNLESS YOU'RE SINGLE AND WITHOUT kids—should involve the whole family. Now, by being involved, I don't mean that one of you earns the money and the others spend it. What I mean is, ideally, every family member should learn to earn, save, spend, budget, and invest.

If your family consists of a husband and wife these helpful how to's can end the Battle of the Budget. Despite the rumors you may have heard, if you co-budget with your husband the world will still respect you in the morning.

Whether you flounder through the financial worries alone or with a spouse, if you have children, you'll want to get them in on the act as well. Later in this chapter we'll talk about training the kids to handle money—yours and theirs. Meanwhile, let's get on with negotiating peace talks in the budget battle.

Sharing the Load

Who wears the financial pants in your family? In many homes budgeting and bookkeeping fall to one person. In the earlier years of our marriage, I landed the job of chief accountant. While my husband looked after investments outside the home, I was responsible for budgets, bills, check statements, bookkeeping, and management of the household. Even though I had the credentials, at times the job seemed overwhelming.

A few years ago, I made my plea for equality and suggested Ron take over a larger share and that we work together for a more peaceful coexistence. You see, we had taken to arguing over who spent what, why, and how much. The tension of my not being aware of his investment ventures and his not being aware of how much it actually cost to run a household often left us both short—short-tempered and short of cash. By working together we could understand each other's problems. Eventually, instead of, "*You* are spending too much money," it became, "*we* are spending too much." With the reconciliation, we not only create compatible budgets, but we share the load.

On the other hand, many of my friends tell me their husbands take care of all the budgeting, bookkeeping, and investing. They are given an allowance for household expenses. If you and your husband are happy with this arrangement, fine. You don't need to change. Remember though, for both your sakes, you should know all the facets of your family's money management program in case you end up on your own.

But are you really happy? Do you ever wonder about the other half of the budget. Do you ever feel like a lone number in an addition problem after the other numbers had been erased? You're not only left with no answer, but without the other part of the problem there's no hope of finding the solution.

Maybe you'd like to play a more significant role in the family's finances, but you think your husband would laugh.

"My husband," Kathy declared, "would say, 'You can't even handle the grocery budget. How do you expect me to turn you loose on mine?'

"Maybe he's right," she sighed. "For years every time he mentioned balancing the budget, the stock market, or investment securities, I threw my mind into automatic pilot. My mouth released an occasional 'Uh-huh, hmmm, oh, that's nice, dear.' I couldn't shift gears until the conversation came back to a more common ground like, 'What's for dinner?' "

I can understand Kathy's hesitation. Let's face it. A woman who has spent the last few years of her life rinsing diapers, wiping noses, and learning that, "goo doo ba dibby dow," means food, will have a rough time making the transition into the sophisticated society of finance. It's hard for a man to take his wife's interest in money seriously when she's been more concerned with the Pablum running down baby's chin than with their money matters.

You can show your husband you are genuinely interested in several ways. First, ask him how you can help keep the budget under control. Second, ask him questions. You could start with that list of things you need to know in chapter 2. Be careful you don't move in too fast. He may wonder if maybe your brains got scrambled instead of his eggs. Oh, and it would be best if you didn't try to impress him with your newly acquired financial lingo like *liquid assets.* He may suspect you are contemplating a spending spree in Italy.

Remember too, your goal is to share, not to have the whole load dumped on you so he can get in a few more hours of leisure time. While we'd all—husbands and wives—like to escape the woes of managing money, especially budgets, it's too big a load for one. Not only that, a one-man (woman) budgeter often finds himself (herself) in the role of the villain, or dictator. Decisions about how money is disbursed lose their bitter taste when made by family consensus.

Now that you and your husband have decided to team up and share the load, let's talk about some goals and game rules.

Teamwork

Your first step in working together as a team will be to set up goals. Maybe your first priority will be to set up a budget you can both live with. Other goals may be teaming up to save for a vacation or a house. Your concerns may be as simple as having enough money left out of your paycheck for groceries. Be sure to set realistic goals for yourselves in order to avoid discouragement. Encourage each other. Know that by extending your marriage contract to include the better and worse of money matters you tie a more secure knot.

Be certain to allow room in that budget for those "little things" that help nurture your relationship. Dinner out, gifts, and time-out trips keep both the romantic and financial side of your marriage running smoothly.

Partnership budgeting and money management requires that you both know the entire financial picture. You don't necessarily have to trade jobs every other month, in fact in many cases that would be impractical. However, you should each take the time to learn about every facet of money management.

Maybe you are just now trying to decide who does what. In that case, write down the various jobs. Budgeting, bookkeeping, checkbook statement, bills, and so on. List the money-related jobs facing your family during the year. Each of you should choose one, then another, until they are all taken. Remember, budgeting, regardless of who got the job of recording, is a joint venture. Sit down as a team to plan it.

You may want to trade off jobs every six months or so. For the last few months, while I've been writing this book, my husband has been kind enough to carry most of the load. The key to teamwork is flexibility. In the trade-off system you have the security of knowing neither your home nor its financial state of affairs will collapse if one of the partners takes a leave of absence.

Whether you choose to keep the same jobs all the time or to trade doesn't matter. What is more important than trading is to be open to each other's problems and needs. Be understanding and develop a spirit of giving.

Yes, I said develop a spirit of giving. Selfishness has done more to trigger the battle of the budget than any other cause.

Suppose Jenny wants a new dress this month and Jim declares his desire for a new set of golf clubs. Their slim budget can't handle both requests. What do they do?

1. Find out exactly how much money can be allotted to these extra items.

2. Determine a need. Can Jim live without his new clubs? Will Jenny suffer undue humility by having absolutely nothing to wear?

3. Come to a mutual agreement. If neither can agree bring up the subject again next month.

4. Do not stubbornly stomp off to the mall and charge it. Your budget will suffer for months and so will your marriage.

5. Think it through and ask yourself, *Is it worth it?*

6. Avoid the whole issue by establishing priorities and setting others' needs above your own.

Once you and your husband have established a teamwork money management system and are co-budgeting happily, it's time to bring in the kids.

Money Matters to Kids Too

"Bring in the kids?" you may stammer. "It's too late. My teenage son thinks a budget is something too heavy to move. My daughter tells me financial freedom is owning her own credit card—in my name."

Ideally, you will have begun your marriage by establishing a budget and money-management partnership. One of your goals should have been to include your children in the family financial responsibilities at an early age. Your principle: to raise up a family of stewards God can be proud of.

However, suppose you missed the ideal and got yourself hopelessly caught in the revolving credit door of life. You are just now in the process of overcoming years of impulse buying and overspending. You nearly lost your head with a case of the credit-card crazies. Now you're coming to your senses. Spending withdrawals hit you only once every couple of months and you can feel the money-hungry habits dropping off your back. The handle you could never get hold of hovers just within your grasp.

If you're just in the process of piecing your financial life back together again, I can understand why you might feel it's too late—but it's not. That is unless your kids have left home. Even then, you still have a chance to provide some wise financial counsel. There's nothing like the testimony of someone who's nearly drowned in an ocean of debts and money troubles to help keep someone else from making the same mistakes.

For those kids still in the nest, tell them it's time for a family council. Sit down with them and explain the financial facts of life. Perhaps they will rebel at the changes, it's a chance you have to take. I won't tell you how to cope with rebellious teenagers in this book, I've already done that in a book called *Have You Hugged Your Teenager Today?* It will help.

But, let's hope your children are understanding and accept the new, budget-wise, you.

Include the children in your family budgeting sessions as early as possible. While you can't expect your four-year-old Michael to fill you in on his profit-and-loss statement for the current fiscal year, he can give you a few pointers on his special needs and where he'd like to vacation this summer.

Even though you can include children in your budget

planning to a small extent, they will have to reach the age of reason before you can expect them to understand how the budget works.

Perhaps you're wondering, *What's the age of reason?*

Good question. We decided our son had reached that magic age when he turned eight.

"Mom!" my son's voice echoed up from behind the radio counter at Sears. "Mom, come quick. Ya gotta see this. It's a radio with a digital clock and snooze alarm so's you won't hav'ta wake me up in the morning. An' see, it's covered with fur so's I can sleep with it. Can I have it?"

As my fingers fumbled with the price tag, my tongue became dry and I shifted nervously. "I'm sorry, honey, but I don't have enough money and your allowance couldn't possibly. . . ."

"Ah Mom, it's only $76, and it's on sale. I could pay a dollar a month."

"No, I'm afraid not. You're too young for a loan. You don't have any collateral. . . ."

My words drifted over his head. "Mom," he brightened, "you don't need any money—just charge it."

His statement washed over me like an ice fog. What had I been teaching my kids? Or maybe I should say, what *hadn't* I taught them? I knew it was time to sit down to a father-mother-son talk about . . . about the financial facts of life. We'd avoided the subject long enough. We wanted time to adjust ourselves. But now it was time to lay all the facts on the table—out in the open.

We talked about checks and how intimately they were related to the amount of money you had in the bank. We told him the bitter truth of lending, and how you shouldn't indulge in credit-card buying unless you were willing to face your responsibilities afterward.

"You always end up paying for your transactions," we cautioned him.

It wasn't easy, letting Dave in on our financial secrets. Once we did, we had no guarantee he wouldn't leak classified information into the neighborhood. I relaxed a little when I realized that our profit-and-loss statement or J. C. Penny bill was not a priority subject in the neighborhood war games, space cadets, and marbles tournaments. Besides, I told him the information he'd received had to be kept from enemy spies. He played a foreign agent, with orders not to divulge his secrets to anyone. One slip of the tongue could mean ... the water gun.

I'm certain you too will feel relief as you step forward and explain the financial facts to your children. Once you've explained that money doesn't grow on trees any more than they arrived by stork, you'll feel a sense of satisfaction. Truth releases the guilt parents feel over those gray areas we somehow can't quite bring ourselves to confess. Discussing finances made me feel good about my communication skills as a parent. Who knows, next year I may even disclose the facts about Santa.

Of course it's a big step, but children have to face facts sometime. There's nothing more shameful for a parent than standing before a teenage interrogation committee demanding the truth about the Tooth Fairy.

When you tell your children about budgets and how to earn and spend money wisely, take it slow. Don't stuff their brains with too much information too quickly. Remember, you're not going to turn your six-year-old into a financial genius in an hour. Be fair. Don't expect to turn the budget over to the kids for at least a month.

Seriously, begin with explanations, like Kim did.

"Mom," called six-year-old Ben. "I need some more allowance. Mine's all runned out."

"No, Ben," Kim explained, "Daddy and I told you your allowance had to last a week."

"Ya, but I spended it, so you gotta gimme some more."

"I'm sorry honey. . . ," Kim began.

"Com'on, Mom," Ben pleaded. "Bret's mom's gonna take us roller skating an' I need fifty cents."

"Ben," Kim asked. "How much money did you have yesterday?"

"A dollar and a half," Ben beamed.

"And what happened to all that money?"

"I told you I spended it. I got candy and pop and a Match Box truck and . . . stuff."

Kim sighed. "And now you don't have any money for skating. That's too bad. I guess you'll have to stay home."

Ben stared at his mother as tears of unbelief trickled down his pouting face.

What a tough lesson. And what better way to teach that all important truth: You can't spend what you don't have.

Allowances

Allowances teach. Or, at least they can, providing you link up the allowance with job responsibility and a budget. A question parents most commonly ask concerning allowances is, "At what age should allowances start?"

If your child seems to have an accurate idea of what money will buy, try a small allowance. Most children at six and over will enjoy handling their own spending money. However, some youngsters, like Annie, may appreciate a different type of reward system.

When Annie's mother heard her offer to a neighborhood friend, she decided an allowance could wait.

"I'll trade you a zillion pennies if I can have two stars and a rainbow sticker," Annie bargained.

"Well, okay," came the reluctant reply.

Rather than give Annie a money allowance, Mom chose to reward her with stars and stickers for jobs well done. At the end of each week or month, the stars and stickers are counted and given monetary value. Under this system Annie can save for a special doll or cash in on an occasional treat.

While Annie may be happy with stars and stickers, other six-year-olds may want to enter the world of high finance. Use your intuition to determine whether your youngsters are ready for allowances.

Once you've determined your child should receive an allowance, you'll probably wonder, *How much should we give?*

Base your youngster's allowance on needs, living expenses, and outside jobs. Consider also, your particular life-style. Be realistic. If you expect eight-year-old Debbie to pay for all her entertainment, books, magazines, hobbies, sports equipment, school activities, lunches and expenses, gifts, and contributions, she'll need more than a dollar a week—unless, like our friend Fran, she's a financial genius.

Sit down with your child and draw up a list of expenses and needs. Then come to terms on an income. You will probably want to correlate allowance to job responsibilities.

If you want to start giving your children their financial wings, let them manage their own money. Not sure where to start? Here are some guidelines. These may help you decide what expenses your kids can handle. By the way, money for these expenses comes from allowance plus wages, depending on capabilities.

- Seven and under: crayons, books, small toys, candy, gum, gifts for their friends, contributions, and savings.
- Ages seven to ten: entertainment, toys, books and magazines, hobbies, school expenses such as games, sports, lunches, supplies, social events, sports equipment, gifts, contributions, and savings.

(From ten and over, the allowance should decrease and outside earnings increase.)

- Ages ten to thirteen: all of the above, plus clothing and upkeep.
- Ages thirteen and over: the above plus personal items for grooming, hair care, cosmetics, transportation expenses including auto, gas, insurance, license fees, traffic

tickets, and may be able to help pay for part of their vacation expenses.

"Wait!" you may be raving. "My ten-year-old can't even remember to take a bath. How can I expect him to budget for school supplies, lunch, and the other items you so casually mentioned?"

I understand—really. While the list of expenses may seem unrealistic for some children, others, like Lisa, who is eight going on twenty, will find it ideal.

As I mentioned, don't expect allowances to cover all the expenses, especially once your youngsters hit ten. Allow what you can or wish, and expect them to work at additional jobs for the rest.

If they can't think of a thing to do, I'm sure you have a few ideas of your own. How about grooming the neighbor's dog—or yard, or selling iced lemonade on a blistery summer day. Should you run short of brainstorms, Malcolm MacGregor's book *Training Your Children to Handle Money* has more moneymaking schemes than the U.S. Patent Office. The book will also give you additional advice on teaching your child the art of money management.

If You Don't Work, You Don't Eat.

One of the hottest questions I hear about allowances is, "Should the allowance be related to household chores?" Years ago, a psychological "expert" convinced me that I should give my children an allowance to cover their needs with no strings attached. My children, naturally, with compassion and cheerful hearts would diligently complete their fair share of the cleaning.

This psychologist obviously had never met a real child. The system wasn't working. One day I took inventory. My kids' need list ran so long I could have wrapped it around the equator. When I told my charming youngsters they had to help with household chores because they lived here and they were expected to do their share, they threatened to move in with Grandma. The idea of an allowance to meet needs and working for nothing seemed unnatural.

After all, in the real world we get paid according to our job performance. If you don't work, you don't eat.

I wasn't sure how to facilitate the change. By paying the kids for every task performed, I'd risk losing my sanity. Can you imagine one of your money-hungry little tyrants dusting the television set four times a day, then demanding payment. Likewise, I would not expect to pay a child for cleaning his or her own room.

The obvious solution for our family fell easily into place. We would use a combination of chores without pay and jobs with earning power. Expected household chores without pay were to include making beds and cleaning rooms, some laundry, and a fair share of dishes and garbage duties.

All other chores, chosen on ability, were assigned. Allowances were based on these jobs. Additional money could be earned by washing windows, cleaning the car, mowing lawns, and so on.

Whatever job responsibilities you attach to allowances, you'll need to take some time out of your busy schedule each week to evaluate. Evaluate job performance and ability to budget. Is Kenny dusting the furniture every week? Did Susy clean the three-month supply of laundry out from under her bed? Does the bathroom tell tales of a fresh cleaning with Pine-Sol or would your guest wonder if you've ever heard of indoor plumbing? Has your cat threatened to find another owner unless you change her litter box?

Although we'd like to put our children on the honor system, it's not practical. We all need periodic evaluations. Evaluations should also be made on the youngster's ability to budget. The budget you drew up to determine how much allowance to give will make a good beginning. Ask your child to write down all expenses each week. Keeping records at this early age will not only help the child live within a budget now, but will, hopefully, become a habit in adulthood.

Keep your child's budget, allowance, and spending experience real. In other words, if tearful Tommy regretfully blew his whole wad down at the ice cream parlor on Monday and has no money for the rest of the week's expenses, what do you do?

You could bail him out, but would that encourage him not to repeat his actions? Would the local banker have that kind of mercy on you? Hardly. While you may wish to make a small advance on the next week's allowance, Tommy will have to undergo a hardship for his impulsive mistake. Be firm, but understanding.

Your goals with allowances are to give your children a taste of the real world of finances and to wean them from dependence to independence.

Teach by Example

Another major way to introduce your child to budget-wise living is by example. Teaching by example can begin at any age. For instance, while you push your grocery cart down the aisles, think aloud. "Hmmm," you may mutter, "turtle eggs have gone up to $2.99 a dozen. Maybe I should substitute chicken eggs. I'd save $2.00."

Or, maybe Jonnie's begging for Fruitie Lutties, the "out-of-orbit" breakfast treat. It promises a galaxy of little stars, planets, rocket ships, and astronauts in bite-sized chunks, already sugar-coated and dipped in fluoride to guard against cavities.

"Look, Jonnie," you explain, as you price it against Heroes, the whole wheat flakes that keep hula-hoopers from losing their pep halfway through competition. "Fruitie Lutties cost $1.39 more than Heroes. We'll buy Heroes and you can tell Daddy how much money we saved."

Little Jonnie will not be impressed. In fact, you'll be lucky if he stops wailing by the time you get to the checkout stand. But, hopefully, your example will be permanently recorded in his subconscious for future reference.

It *does* work. Our son Dave, at thirteen, came home with a super bargain. He had been wanting a guitar. By comparison shopping, we found we could get a beginner for about $40. He'd just started saving for it when he chanced upon a neighborhood garage sale. A "hardly used" guitar beckoned him from its lonely corner and displayed a price of $15. David, having been taught comparison shopping and negotiating, offered $10. "It's all I've got," he said. The seller agreed. What a buy. It carried him through two years of lessons and moved on to our daughter. It still finds its way to outings, youth groups, and camp fires where the more sophisticated models daren't venture.

"Train up a child in the way he should go: and when he is old, he will not depart from it" (Proverbs 22:6). This well-worn proverb has mostly been used in books on raising kids. Money management is an area that should receive as much importance as behavioral management. Both areas need discipline. When we come down to basics, that is what budgeting is—discipline.

You and I will probably agree. It is much harder to discipline yourself in adulthood if you were not taught the art as a child. So do your children a favor. Train them up in the way they should go—toward discipline in money management.

In Addition

Along with allowances and examples, there are a few additional points I'd like to make about family budgeting.

1. Show the kids the give-and-take philosophy of a budget. For example, money for the extras like a vacation to Hawaii, may be saved by not eating for a month. Or, they can take part in cutting out snacks; offering a percentage of their allowance; more frugal use of electricity, school paper, and supplies; spending less on clothing; and so on.

Likewise, if your clothes-crazy Carla wants to spend $40 on a designer shirt, she'll have to give up some of the less important items in her budget such as the championship football game, the ski trip to Mount Bachelor, or the senior prom.

2. Don't argue over money and don't blame your spending habits on the kids. One ulcer in the family is enough. Perhaps the kids *are* a strain on the budget, but it's not their fault. Sudden and continuous growth spurts make it hard to keep them in clothes, and food bills soar in the presence of growing teenage boys. Bickering over who unbalances the budget won't solve the problem.

3. Taking part in the goals and planning of the family budget gives children a feeling of importance. Self-esteem builds as they see their opinions and suggestions listened to, weighed, discussed, and sometimes used. Family budgeting can build family unity.

4. Get your older children in on the action of record keeping. The partnership program could easily include your teenager. A turn at keeping records and working with a family budget gives the youngster a look at what he or she will face in the future.

Dale and Edna came up with an interesting answer for their demanding teenager.

"Why can't we buy the Olson's sailboat, Dad? It's only $30,000," sixteen-year-old Todd grumbled. "Everybody's got one but us."

"The Olson's won't, after they sell theirs."

"That's different. Mr. Olson lost his job and they can't make the payments. Besides," Todd added, "you've got money."

"I'll tell you what, son," Dale calmly approached his son. "Here is my paycheck, the checkbook, the bills, and the budget. You figure it all out for the next couple of months. Write the checks and I'll sign them. If you can come up with a better way of handling the money, fine. See if you can squeeze payments for a sailboat out of it."

"Wow! Thanks, Dad," exclaimed the confident lad.

Excellent experience for a teen, don't you think? Interestingly enough, the subject of the sailboat mysteriously sank under the reality of keeping the budget afloat.

Money is important to your kids. Whether you teach purposefully or choose to ignore the subject, they will learn. They will either learn the art of spending frivolously and foolishly, or prudently with discernment. You set the example, the choice is yours.

16

Records, Taxes, and Tears

ALONG WITH BUDGETING COMES RECORD KEEPING, and that brings up the subject of taxes, which brings me to the point of tears. Every year, I resolved to keep better records. And, every year, tax time found me in a puddle of tears as I sorted through stacks of receipts I'd tossed in a drawer.

Tax time tears, I'm happy to say, are a thing of the past. Not because I've become a fantastically organized bookkeeper, but because I've come to accept my personality and chosen a record-keeping system tailor-made for me.

I encourage you to do the same. In the next few pages we'll talk about the why's of record keeping. Then I'll offer five building-block recording systems, beginning at the most basic and working up in complexity. But first, consider the whys.

Why Keep Records?

Obviously, records make you aware of your financial situation or condition. Then comes a more important reason for records—Uncle Sam.

In other words, if you don't keep accurate and up-to-date accounts of your income and outgo, you may find yourself in San Quentin. But, at least there you'd have plenty of time to learn and no excuses not to. The government induces us to record income and expenses so they can collect their fair share.

We also keep records to account for our spent money. This is especially true if you maintain a checking account. Bankers frown on the practice of writing checks on a zero or minus balance. It's unlawful.

Besides keeping you out of jail, faithful recording can keep you from the poorhouse. It is a well-known fact that budgeting and recording reduce the risk of overspending.

How you choose to keep those records is entirely up to you. We all have varied life-styles, personalities, and incomes. Naturally, some will want to keep more detailed records than others. So, let's get on with finding a method just for you.

Toss-It-in-a-Drawer-Till-Tax-Time Tilly

I've started with the simplest, most basic system. It's the one I call Toss-it-in-a-drawer-till-tax-time. This is dedicated to gals like Tilly, who believe numbers were created for the sole purpose of confusing them.

It also serves as a great system for women who lead super busy lives and haven't gotten around to being a "total woman" organizationally.

Tilly's method can work, but only on the tax records, which can be put on hold for a year at a time. Even with this most simplified method, you can't escape the monthly bill paying and checkbook duties.

Here is how it works:

1. Reserve a drawer or file folder. In it, toss all the receipts collected during the year for tax purposes. This includes pay stubs, completed bank statements with cancelled checks, cash and charge receipts. For a list of deductions you'll want to save receipts for, see page 175 of this chapter.

2. At the year's end, haul out your stuffed drawer or file and dump it on the floor or table.

3. Begin the sorting process. For most households, the job should take no more than about four hours. More complex households, however, with small businesses, rental properties, or other investments, may find this sort-and-record session lasting up to four days. To simplify the job, file the receipts in an accordion file folder or in envelopes.

4. Total, clip, and staple each category and record the title and total on top for easy reading.

5. Record your totals on a worksheet.

6. Give yourself a standing ovation.

7. Call your tax preparer for an appointment. Or, wait a few days and do it yourself.

Tilly's isn't a bad method. Of course, you may feel slight to moderate (maybe even heavy) remorse come January. The secret of successful "toss-iters" is attitude. Accept the fact that this method is your choice. You have exchanged small increments of time during the year for one lump sum at the end.

Approach it in a cheerful, matter-of-fact manner. You may want to begin positive mind preparation as early as October or November. Repeat phrases like, "I'm really looking forward to sitting down with that pile of papers." Give yourself affirmations. Positive statements repeated often enough might actually make you believe what you said.

Ideas From Once-a-Month Martha

Suppose the toss-it idea, no matter how much you enjoyed that year-long freedom from records, leaves you feeling like a cross between a hunted rabbit and a wounded rhino come January. You are either bouncing off the walls for fear the IRS will nab you for tax evasion, or you're so growly, the family fears you'll charge. Maybe, no matter how hard you tried, you couldn't find happiness with a year's worth of bookkeeping to do at one time.

I understand. Here is an idea that might let you continue your drawer-stuffing technique and still cut the January work load.

Since you are bound by your bill collectors to slip into the role of bill payer and bank statement balancer once a month, why not follow Martha's example. Use that time more efficiently. Add half an hour to your task.

Wait! Before you tell me your time budget has been stretched too far already, read on. You're sitting at a desk or table anyway, right? After you pay the bills and come to an agreement with the bank's computer over your checkbook, open the infamous receipt drawer. By the way, if you start this new system in January, you won't have to make up lost time.

1. Label envelopes or file folders with *Income, Mortgage, Telephone, Utilities,* and so on. (Use the item list from your budget form in chapter 13.) Do include nondeductible items such as groceries and clothing to help you with your budget totals.

2. Place all cancelled checks, statements, and other receipts into the corresponding folders.

Once the initial files are set up, filing the receipts each month will take only minutes.

If you don't own a file cabinet and can't afford one, a

sturdy shoe box will suffice. Or, if you want something in-between, purchase a prelabeled, accordion-type file folder. A variety store near me has one called the 21-Pocket Data File costing $6.97.

By giving an extra few minutes a month, you'll completely eliminate the troublesome task of transforming a pile of papers into a recognizable list of income and deductions in January. All your receipts will be in presorted categories and all you'll have to do is run totals, record them on a worksheet, and they're ready for the tax form.

File Systems and Checkbook Records for Organized Ora

In this system all remnants of the toss-it technique disappear. This more organized style utilizes the mystique of Martha's files and adds a detailed checkbook record.

My friend Ora uses her checkbook to record all of her expenses. Ora writes checks or uses a credit card for nearly all expenses. She makes an entry in her check register at the time of purchase. All receipts—cash and charge—find their way into a checkbook pocket. Here is Ora's method.

1. Once a week, Ora chose Thursday evening, transfer your cash and charge receipts to the appropriate file.
2. When you balance your checkbook at the end of each month, pull out the cancelled checks and file them.

A simple method, yes, but the secret of success lies in keeping a clean and accurate check register. With it you'll be able to set up a more accurate budget and maybe even balance with the bank statement at the end of the month.

Ora's check register looks like this:

PLEASE BE SURE TO DEDUCT ANY PER CHECK CHARGES OR SERVICE CHARGES THAT MAY APPLY TO YOUR ACCOUNT

CHECK NO.	DATE	CHECK ISSUED TO OR DESCRIPTION OF DEPOSIT	(−) AMOUNT OF CHECK	√ TAX ITEMS	(−) CHECK FEE (IF ANY)	(+) AMOUNT OF DEPOSIT	BALANCE 152.30
Jan		*Jim's Salary Income*				*500.00*	*652.30*
2430	*1/3*	*First Federal Mortgage*	*220.00*				*220.00* *432.30*
2431	*1/3*	*P.U.D. Utilities*	*22.00*				*22.00* *408.30*
2432	*1/3*	*N. W. Natural Gas Utilities*	*15.00*				*15.00* *393.30*
2433	*1/6*	*Community Church tithe*	*70.00*				*70.00* *323.30*
2434		*1st Savings & Loan Savings*	*25.00*				*25.00* *298.30*
2435	*1/7*	*Danny allowance*	*11.00*				*11.00* *287.30*
2436	*1/10*	*Mervyn's Clothing*	*13.37*				*13.37* *273.92*
2437	*1/10*	*Albertson's groceries*	*88.72*				*88.72* *186.20*
2438	*1/12*	*Allstate (2nd Paymt.) Car Insurance*	*52.00*				*52.00* *134.20*
	1/15	*Jim's paycheck Income*				*500.00*	*634.20*
2439	*1/16*	*Safeway Groc. 116.43/Cash: 20.00*	*136.43*				*136.43* *497.77*
2440	*1/16*	*Clark College Art Class tuition/Education*	*54.00*				*54.00* *443.77*

REMEMBER TO RECORD AUTOMATIC PAYMENTS / DEPOSITS ON DATE AUTHORIZED.

At tax time Ora tallies all deductible expenses and lists them neatly on a columnar pad headed: *Tax Records.* It's so neat, Ora's tax person sends her flowers. (See example on page 169.)

TAX RECORDS		
Item	Income	Expense
Salary: Jim	*14,440.00*	
Ora (see W-2 forms attached)	*6,000.00*	
Interest Income: First Fed.	*143.80*	
Pacific First Federal	*386.39*	
Expenses: Medical		*267.30*
Dental		*342.00*
Contributions		*340.00*
Union dues		*300.00*
Uniforms—Nursing		*126.88*
5/18/ *Casualty loss—1972 Toyota net loss*		*750.00*

General Ledgers, Journals, and Diaries

Don't let the titles turn you away in tears. It's not that difficult. In fact, Ora's tax record is a simple ledger. I'm going to teach you a basic, home-bookkeeping system, and you can build it up any way you choose. If you've a flare for numbers and love to play with your assets and liabilities, debits, credits, and have the time, set yourself up with a complete set of books. Enjoy!

Most modern homemakers have little time to play with numbers. Many of you have a job away from home or are involved with your own business. And quite possibly, like me, you find your record-keeping requirements have become more than what Toss-it-in-a-drawer-till-tax-time can offer. Perhaps you need or prefer totals of your expenses at the end of each month. If so, that's where ledgers, journals, and diaries come in.

A ledger or journal refers to a columnar, ruled paper on which you transfer your receipts of income and expenses. The worksheet you prepared for budgeting was, in fact, an unrefined journal. With ledgers and journals, you reap the benefits of a one- or two-page account of expenses and income instead of a drawer or file full of receipts.

Let's begin with a ledger. It's a simple two-column sheet on which records of single accounts are kept. Say for example you wanted to keep a separate account of groceries or clothing. Here is a sample from my ledger.

ADDRESS CLOTHING | NAME BUDGETED AMOUNT $80.00

MEMO | TERMS | LIMIT | ACCOUNT NO. | SHEET NO.

DATE		ITEM	FOL	✓	DEBIT	CREDIT	BALANCE
Jan		*Bal Forward*					42 00
		Mervyns Swimsuit				15 00	27 00
		Budget Jan			80 00		107 00
	15	*J.C. Pennys Nylons*				4 50	102 50
	15	*Nordstrome Dress*				46 00	56 50
		CY's House of samples. Misc				42 00	14 50
		Totals			80 00	107 50	14 50
Feb	*1*	*Bal. Forward*					14 50
		Budget Feb.			80 00		94 50

The ledger is an excellent way of keeping track of cash allowances. In other words, if you draw out $150 every two weeks to cover groceries, a ledger helps you to keep close account of your budgeted money.

A journal can save you time with year-end tax records if you add a smidgen more time to your bookkeeping job each month. It also helps you with your budgeting. In fact, I've mapped out a simple journal that tells you at the end of the month whether or not you over- or underspent your income. (As if you needed paper to tell you.) This journal is called a Cash Disbursement Journal, which is just a fancy name for cash in, cash out, cash out, cash out.

You can buy journals already headed, or do-it-yourself columnar pads. I prefer the columnar pads, so I can choose my own headings. (See page 172.)

My Appointmentbook/Diary proves its value every day. I use it to enter mileage, business meals, as well as other var-

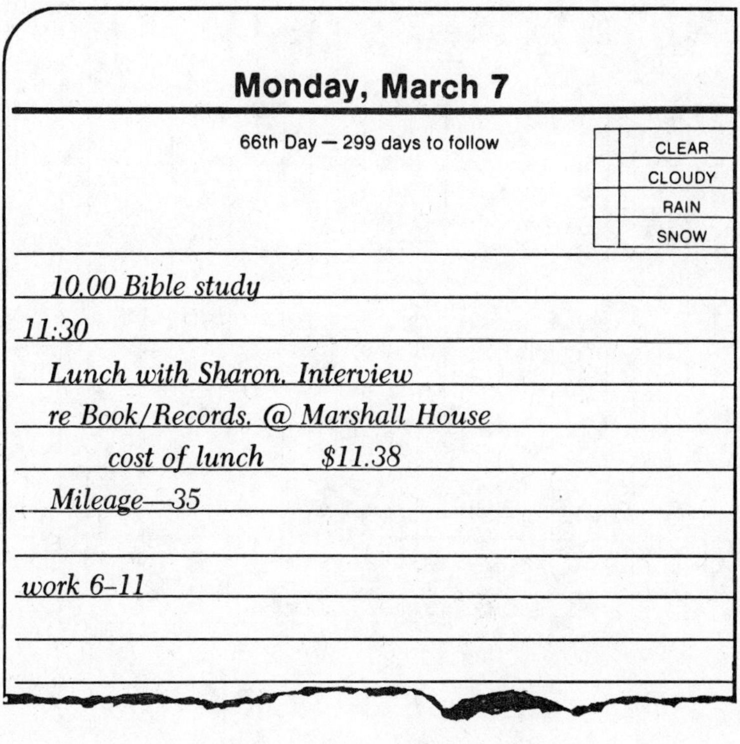
Monday, March 7

66th Day — 299 days to follow

CLEAR
CLOUDY
RAIN
SNOW

10.00 Bible study

11:30

Lunch with Sharon. Interview

re Book/Records. @ Marshall House

cost of lunch $11.38

Mileage—35

work 6–11

MONTHLY CASH DISBURSEMENT JOURNAL—January

EXPENSES	wk #1	wk #2	wk #3	wk #4	Monthly Totals
TITHES, CONTRIBUTIONS	*$ 60.00*	*$ 60.00*	*$ 60.00*	*$ 60.00*	*$ 240.00*
SAVINGS	*25.00*	*75.00*			*100.00*
MORTGAGE	*250.00*		*200.00*		*450.00*
UTILITIES		*30.00*			*30.00*
TELEPHONE			*18.00*		*18.00*
FOOD				*300.00*	*300.00*
CLOTHING			*35.00*		*35.00*
INSURANCE			*38.00*		*38.00*
TRANSPORTATION	*28.00*	*65.00*	*32.00*	*28.00*	*153.00*
MEDICAL				*45.00*	*45.00*
DENTAL					
PERSONAL	*12.00*				*12.00*
ENTERTAINMENT					
EDUCATION					
MISC		(TAXES)	*60.00*		*60.00*
TOTAL EXPENSES	*$375.00*	*$230.00*	*$443.00*	*$433.00*	*$1481.00*
INCOME					
A) SALARY	*500.00*	—	*500.00*	*500.00*	*1500.00*
B) RENTAL INCOME	—	*350.00*	—	—	*350.00*
TOTAL INCOME	*$500.00*	*$350.00*	*$500.00*	*$500.00*	*$1850.00*
MINUS TOTAL EXPENSES	*375.00*	*230.00*	*443.00*	*433.00*	*1481.00*
TOTAL BALANCE	*$125.00*	*$120.00*	*$ 57.00*	*$ 67.00*	*$ 369.00*

ious expenses. It can serve as a ledger as well as tell me where I'm going and where I've been. Believe me there are days when my body may be dutiful but my brain has retired to the pasture. See page 171 for a sample of my diary.

Home Computers

This style of high-technology record keeping fits a wide variety of personalities. Women who love numbers and detail, as well as women who, at times, feel totally mindless, will be comfortable with computers. Once programmed, the machine saves time, energy (yours), and brain power. About the only thing a computer doesn't save is an already distraught budget. I'd love to dump my record keeping into a computer and let it handle my money affairs. Some computers can be programmed to budget, balance checkbooks—*Hmmm. With my own computer I could even the odds with the bank*—pay bills, and fill out tax forms. Computers plan menus and even spit out corresponding grocery lists.

Kathy, a friend, bought an Apple home computer and cheered. "It's a miracle. Besides keeping perfect records, the games entertain the kids for hours."

With a miracle machine like that, who needs journals, checkbooks, or even receipts stuffed in a drawer? Exciting as computers may seem, they are not perfect. Ask Kathy.

Last December an ice storm knocked out power all over east Vancouver. Kathy's computer lost its memory—*she* forgot to transfer her records onto a permanent disk. A year's worth of budgets, balances, and bills paid disappeared as "Apple" popped, snorted, wheezed, whined, and died. Poor Kathy, how was she to know. "I never *could* follow directions," she cried. "It was like losing my last set of keys down a bottomless pit."

Fortunately, before her home computer days, Kathy had perfected the "Toss-it . . ." record-keeping method. Her . . . ah . . . filing system paid off. As a matter of habit, she routinely tossed receipts and so on in a drawer. All she had to do was sort through them.

Tax Records—What to Keep

With the help of an accountant, I've compiled a list of receipts the average family will need to file or record for tax purposes. To save you confusion, because the list is a long one, mark those items applying to you with a yellow marker.

INCOME—list all income

- Salary—head of household
- Salary—spouse

  These records must include total wages, federal tax withheld, FICA, state and local taxes. Most of this information should appear on your W-2 form, which your employer will mail to you no later than January 31.
- Alimony received (excluding child support)
- Interest and Dividend Income
- Income from sale of property, stocks, mutual funds, etc.
  - A. Short term (property or investments held one year or less)
  - B. Capital gains (property or investments held more than one year)
- Royalties, Commissions, and Fees
- Bonuses and Prizes
- Tips and Gratuities
- Annuities and Pension Income
- Lump Sum Distribution from Retirement Plans
- Unemployment Compensation (Note even though it may not be taxable.)
- Social Security Benefits
- Veteran's Benefits
- Workman's Compensation
- Other Income:__________

You are legally bound by the government to keep documentation of all incomes. With most of the above you will be given a statement or W-2 form. File them. With others, such as tips, keep a daily record, like a diary.

EXPENSES—TAXABLE DEDUCTIONS

- Adoption Expenses
- Alimony Paid
- Casualty Losses—Losses include auto accidents, fire, theft, storms, property damage, etc. List the loss, the value, and insurance payment.
- Charitable Work—Document expenses such as transportation, special clothing, and food and lodging if out of town.
- Childcare and Dependent Care Expenses—Baby-sitting services
- Contributions—tithes and offerings—list the name of the organization, and the amount. Keep a receipt or cancelled check.
- Doctors and Dentists—This includes the amount of the bill as well as transportation or mileage on all trips.
- Finance Charges on Contracts
- Interest Paid—on all loans or mortgages
- Investment Expenses—Include supplies, publications, transportation, cost of safe-deposit box.
- Job-Related Expenses—Employee expenses could include auto, special shoes, tools, uniforms, union dues, education expenses, professional dues and journals, safety equipment, transportation to a second job, job-seeking expenses, and employment agency fees.
- Medical Insurance—premiums
- Medications and Drugs—Include prescriptions, vitamins and diet supplements if prescribed, and over-the-counter drugs such as aspirin, acetaminophen, cough syrup, etc.

- Other Medical Expenses—Include acupuncture, chiropractors, practitioners, nursing care, convalescent centers, special schools for physically or mentally handicapped, and transportation to and from. Also include any costs for ambulances, artificial limbs, eyeglasses, eye exams, hearing aids and batteries, lab tests, rental of equipment, supportive or corrective devices, therapy, and X rays.
- Service Charges and Carrying Charges—on credit cards, cash reserves, etc.
- Taxes—Include income, sales, state, and estimated taxes paid during the year.
- Tax Preparation Costs.

Keeping track of these expenses and deductions isn't the overwhelming job it may seem. Simply keep in a file, or a drawer if you wish, all the cancelled checks, paid invoices, receipts, or other papers that show your deductible expenses. You will need to keep these records and receipts for seven years after the due date for filing your income tax.

These deductions are for the average household. If your family runs a business or is into high finance, you may need more information. If so, see a tax accountant or an IRS representative.

This is stuff Uncle Sam says we should keep records on, if we are going to take deductions and save money on our taxes. Of course, you don't have to bother.

You could fill out the simple tax form and let the government take its large chunk. It's *your* money. Personally, I prefer to take full advantage of the deductions the government offers. Your savings could mean a vacation to the south of France, or a college education. On the other hand, your savings may not even be enough to buy a ticket to the Tax Cutter's Ball. In that case, skip it. Try again next year. In the meantime, check into the tax advantages such as I.R.A. or

Keogh accounts. I'm sure you can find more exciting ways to use your money than Uncle Sam.

Taxes, Taxes, Who Does the Taxes?

Now that we know what the IRS requires for filing tax forms, let's talk about who's going to fill out the forms. Maybe you are thinking about doing them yourself. Sure. You can do your own taxes. You can also pull your own teeth. The project thrills me about as much as eating watermelon in a sandstorm.

Why? Well, for one thing, it takes years of training to develop an aptitude for the technicalities of our tax system. The last time we had our taxes done, our accountant took out three different notebooks, each four inches thick, to help us decide how to fill out the forms to our best tax advantage. I have neither the time nor the desire to do my own taxes.

But then, if you like a challenge and you don't think the IRS will challenge you, here's your plan of attack. The Internal Revenue Service puts out a book called *Your Federal Income Tax*, which you can obtain from your local IRS office. With some intense study and concentration you can pull it off. You're on your own. Good luck!

Suppose you're more like me and would just as soon resist the temptation to tackle the taxes alone. Who do you go to for help? First of all, let's take a look at the tax preparation agencies.

The problems I've encountered with these agencies is that the tax preparer is not always an expert. In fact, some of them are students who, until they took a crash course in tax forms, knew no more than you. While they are not all totally incompetent, their credentials as well as their expertise in the tax game vary greatly.

We recently suffered through the ordeal of finding the right person for the job. We finally found a fellow who called his firm Accuracy Unlimited. The name should have aroused suspicions, but when you're desperate. . . . When the completed forms came back for Ron and me to sign, we found no less than fifteen obvious errors. The IRS found two more. A year I'd like to forget.

Fortunately, our search ended when we found Karen, a certified public accountant—an expert. We need her to make sure we've taken all possible deductions. She's a treasure. In addition, should the IRS question an entry or decide to audit, the CPA can represent you, whereas, the tax preparer can't.

Whether you choose a CPA or a tax preparer, find one you can trust, and one who will work in your best interests.

Even though someone else may fill out your tax forms, you are the one responsible for getting the right information to your agent. Have your papers in order by using one of the bookkeeping systems provided for you in this chapter. It will save you and your agent time and save you money.

Besides, dumping a year's supply of receipts on your accountant's desk is rather like airing your dirty laundry in public. Not nice. Not nice at all.

Can you believe it? Tax records was the last item on my agenda for this tedious and brain-stretching section. Now it's time for the tears. I called this chapter "Records, Taxes, and Tears," remember? I don't know how you feel after reading about all this work, but after writing about it I'm going to have a good cry. I may even throw in a nervous breakdown for good measure.

But as all good things must come to an end, so must tears. I feel a little guilty because someone just reminded me to do as Paul advises in James and "count it all joy." We've been counting and counting and counting, but I lost the joy.

All is not lost, however, because I think we can reap joy in the seventeenth and final chapter. Join me as we climb the mountain to financial freedom.

Ahhh! We're smiling already.

17
Financial Freedom

FINANCIAL FREEDOM! HAS A NICE RING TO IT, DON'T you think? What does *financial freedom* mean to you?

"If I were financially free," dreamed Sarah, "I could go anywhere, buy anything, and never worry about overspending."

"To me," Jill said, "financial freedom means security. Having enough money to live comfortably for the rest of my life."

"It's never having money problems," mused Karen.

These were among the most common answers I received when I asked the question, "What is financial freedom?"

Most women's definitions refer to the dependency on money to supply their needs. Enough money will solve the problem, give security, and produce a carefree life.

As we define financial freedom let's take a look at its opposite—financial slavery. When I looked at the phrase I thought, *Aha. If freedom means emancipate, unshackle, and free from bondage, then financial freedom must mean free from the bondage of money. When money has no control over my life, I will have achieved financial freedom.* With the light of true financial freedom in our minds, let's begin our climb up the jagged trail to the mountaintop exhilaration of financial freedom. The first plateau will be hardest to reach. It is in this climb you learn to live unshackled.

What Price Freedom?

One of the saddest stories in the Bible is in Luke 18, where Jesus tells the rich young ruler, "Sell all that you have and distribute it to the poor, and you will have treasure in heaven; and come, follow me." The young man turned sadly away. The cost of discipleship was too great.

"How hard it is for those who have riches to enter the kingdom of God," Jesus then said. "For it is easier for a camel to go through the eye of a needle than for a rich man to enter the kingdom of God" (vv. 22–25).

Examples like these make me shudder. I feel like saying, "Sure, God, ah . . . who needs money. I . . . ah . . . I'll just play it safe and stay poor. That way I won't be tempted to love money more than I love You."

Unfortunately, being poor doesn't save us from the love of or lust for money and material things. In fact, the love of money has caused greed, slander, murder, and as the Bible says, "all evils," in rich and poor alike (1 Timothy 6:10 RSV).

So what is the Bible saying, that it's sinful to be rich? Hardly. Some of God's most faithful servants were extremely wealthy men. Take Abraham, for example, and Jacob, David, Solomon, and Job.

Job had the attitude toward God and money in the right perspective. And that attitude is what we need to develop in order to reach the first plateau in our climb to financial freedom.

How did Job feel about money? After God allowed Satan to destroy all that he had, Job remained faithful. "Then Job arose, and rent his robe, and shaved his head, and fell upon the ground, and worshiped. And he said, 'Naked I came from my mother's womb, and naked shall I return; the Lord gave, and the Lord has taken away; blessed be the name of the Lord.' In all this Job did not sin or charge God with wrong" (Job 1:20–22 RSV).

Job teaches some important principles. First, I have nothing unless God gives it to me. Second, all things belong to God. This is repeated over and over in the Bible. In Psalms 50:12 (RSV) God says, ". . . for the world and all that is in it is mine."

The third and possibly most important principle is to keep focused on the Lord and be faithful regardless of our circumstances.

Money, whatever the amount, is entrusted to us from God. We are His stewards or agents. What a responsibility. We can use it to build up ourselves, or to glorify God. We can build up our estates and hoard our treasures, or we can give generously to enhance the Lord's work.

The more money we have, the more we need to pray for God's special gift of giving. My friend Lauraine told me, "My goal is to outgive God. I know it's impossible," she laughed, "but think how good it will feel to try."

The impossibilities are as endless as a rainbow. Since God provides us with everything we have, what do we have to lose? As God's agents, we are to put *all* that God gives us to good use. Then He asks that we return only 10 percent as a tithe. This is really amazing when you think about it. If you handled money for a wealthy man—you invested it and acted as his agent—you would probably only get 10 percent for your time and talent. God gives you 90 percent. When I think of tithing in that way, I feel embarrassed.

Actually, ashamed is probably a better word. You see, there have been times when I had so many bills I thought of tithing as a burden. What I'd really like to do is come to the place where I could turn it around. I'd give God 90 percent and live on 10 percent. As I look at my present financial situation that could take a while.

While 90 percent may be an unrealistic goal at present, my husband and I have set our sights on 20 to 30 percent within the next two years. This means we must eliminate all outstanding debts, live more simply (meet our needs not wants), live within our means (money left after the tithes and taxes), and invest carefully.

You have reached the first plateau in your climb to financial freedom and wise money management when you name and claim these principles for your life:

1. I acknowledge God's ownership of all that I have.

2. I am a steward of God's property. I want everything I earn and spend to glorify Him.

3. A tithe is my public acknowledgment of my belief in God as Lord and Master—Owner of all.

4. I will keep my heart and mind focused on my Lord. He holds eternal treasures. "For where your treasure is, there will your heart be also" (Matthew 6:21 RSV).

5. I consider money as a tool or instrument by which God can achieve His will on earth—a method by which God meets our needs.

Now, supposing you, the woman of the house, have accepted the Lord's ownership and your responsibility to tithe; but your husband hasn't. In that case, submit to his will and pray. You might also want to leave a couple of valuable books, like this one, laying around that could cause him to reevaluate. Other good books include *Your Money Matters,* by Malcolm MacGregor, and *You Can Beat the Money Squeeze,* by George and Marjean Fooshee.

Once you reach the first plateau, you can take a much-needed rest. Stay as long as it takes you to be free, to unshackle those chains that bind you and send them hurling over the nearest cliff. This first plateau represents a key that unlocks the secrets of financial success. It also lays the groundwork and becomes the foundation upon which our future—whether we are wealthy, poor, or somewhere between—is built.

Of course, it is possible to hire a chopper, skip that initial climb, and proceed to the second phase of our journey. But be forewarned. A mountain can get pretty shakey without a firm foundation. Remember Mount St. Helen, the "dormant" volcano? An unstable foundation produced devastating results.

With a secure base camp behind us, I suggest we move on up the mountain to the next plateau.

Provide and Conquer

Our goal is freedom—freedom from the dependency on money and freedom from money worries. We move on to achieve part of that goal on the second plateau. Provide the necessities, such as food, clothing, and shelter. That seems relatively simple, doesn't it? We've been providing for the needs of our families for years.

I wish I could let you ascend that quickly, but I can't. You'll notice the subtitle reads "Provide and Conquer." In order to conquer this second phase of our journey we should be able to answer yes to the following questions.

1. Does your present income provide for your family's needs? Not wants, but *needs.*

2. Do you have a small store of extra food, water, and fuel in case of a crisis?

3. Do you have three to six months' worth of your income (minus taxes) in a secure and liquid, or easily accessible, savings account in case of an emergency?

4. Do you have adequate life and medical insurance?

5. Have you set up a retirement fund?

As you may have guessed, this area of financial growth is centered on provision. I talked about provision and the importance of savings accounts in chapter 13. You may want to go back and refresh your memory.

Many people never get beyond this plateau in their financial life. Let's face it. Some of us are better equipped to handle money matters and the art of high finance than others. However, I see the completion of this phase as necessary in order to avoid the pitfalls of worry and anxiety over financial affairs. These priorities should be met before we start the third phase of our journey up the mountain toward financial freedom.

Growth and Development

If you will recall, in chapter 13, we explored the Land of Investments. It is in this area we reach the third plateau in our quest for financial freedom.

In this region we begin investment programs that will make a profit for the Lord's money.

Money market funds, certificates of deposit, Treasury Bills, and mutual funds are highly recommended for this growing area. Real estate is also a growth investment. Be aware that although many of these investments offer growth, there is always a potential risk.

By investigating thoroughly before you invest, you reduce your risks. Know the market.

Many people settle here. Wise investing in this rich and fertile plateau brings financial security without the risks found in climbing to the top. And since some investors are more knowledgeable and surefooted than others this is good.

Once you've acknowledged God's ownership of your finances, His partnership in all of your financial endeavors, the benefits and importance of tithing, made provisions for your family (relations), and are earning extra income on your "growth" investments, you are ready to take risks.

Taking Risks With the Master's Money

God is not against our taking risks, even when it comes to money. The parable of the talents in Matthew 25:14–30 tells us that. When the servants doubled their money, and you know high-yield investments are high-risk, the Master was pleased. Would He have been pleased if the whole bundle had been lost? I wonder.

I'd like to think that if either of these successful servants had invested as wisely and prayerfully as they knew how, and lost, the Master would have been quick to forgive. But a foolish speculation?

God wants us to be cautious in our investments. After all, we're taking risks with His money. Prayer and study should be a prerequisite for heading into any type of investment.

Do you have an overabundance of money that you feel you could risk on higher-yield investments? Have you completed the requirements of the first, second, and third plateaus? Then perhaps you are in a position to diversify some of that money into speculative stocks and bonds, gas and oil, precious metals and stones, and so on.

The more money we have, the more we can give. Remember the goal to outgive God. As Christians and God's stewards, we must establish goals to help us in our climb to financial freedom. Our priorities must be clear, to provide for our families, our Christian friends in need, and others in need. When God is an intricate part of our financial life, we can break the bonds that hold us to money and the worry it brings.

Can We Ever Be Financially Free?

What a difficult mountain to climb. Even though my husband and I have invested in the growth areas of the third plateau and dabbled in the fields of the high country, we have had to come back down the mountain. Our foundation needed work. I'm afraid we are still building on that base and, if I'm not mistaken, we will always be strengthening and remodeling that base as we grow in God's Word and through prayer.

Where did you find yourself on the mountain of financial freedom? Do you, like me, have to go back to base camp and straighten out priorities?

I used to think of financial freedom as did some of the women at the first part of this chapter. *If only I had enough money, I could. . . .*

But now, financially free means:

- Freedom to invest in people—both time and money for the glory of God.
- Freedom to give generously when I am abundantly blessed.
- Freedom to receive when I am poor.
- Freedom from conceit, pride, and anxiety, regardless of whether I'm rich or poor.
- Freedom to be content, whatever my situation.
- Freedom to be what God wants me to be—no strings attached.

Hmmm. ". . . no strings. . . ." No earthly treasures to bind me on earth—that's emancipation. But could I? If God cut the strings that tied me to my home, my car, my clothes, my potter's wheel, my typewriter, and said, "Sell all that you have and distribute to the poor, and you will have treasure in heaven; and come, follow me," could I? Or, would I scramble frantically, trying to retie those strings and make some sort of order out of the chaos in my heart. Could I stand to lose all this "stuff" I've gathered?

Once a woman, Sarah, came home from a meeting. As she pulled up into her driveway, she viewed what had once filled her life. Before her stood a black, charred, ash-filled foundation of what had once been her home. In that tragic night, flames had consumed her husband, her children, and all that she had except the clothes she wore.

Sometimes, when I become too attached to a thing or to money, I think of Sarah. I ask myself, could I give this up? Several years ago I became so involved with my pottery, I didn't think I could let it go. I poured and molded myself into it; I spent days and nights in the wonder of creating. One day I felt as if God asked me the question, "Could you give it up for Me?"

I cried and realized how tightly I'd tied the string. Then I said, "Yes, Lord, but I'll need Your help."

God showed me other areas of interest and helped me get my passion for pottery under control. In just that way God can help us overcome a passion for money and what it can buy.

Financial freedom isn't an illusive dream. It is possible to be free, but only through a right relationship with a loving God, who shows us the way. Through prayer and study in the Bible, we can find our place on the mountain of financial freedom.

Congratulations!

Wherever you are in your climb to financial freedom, I want you to stop and give yourself a standing ovation. Why? Because you are to be congratulated. After reading this book, you can now consider yourself a six on the Financial Genius Scale. Not only that, you are now a Financially Aware Woman.

There has been so much to learn, and if you haven't absorbed it all yet, don't worry. It takes time. Perhaps you are wondering why you only get a six and not an eight or a ten. That's a good question.

Since I wrote this book for women as an introduction to money management, I'm sure you'll understand. I wrote the book, and you can't have a higher score than the author.

I encourage you to move on. You are now ready to tackle some of the books written by tens, like Fran, and like Venita VanCaspel (*The Power of Money Dynamics*). Their words will no longer make you feel like a goose on Swan Lake. And, while as sixes we are still a long way from the Financial Genius Award, we have gathered many practical and usable ideas. We can carry these ideas into our daily financial dealings, whether we buy a field like the virtuous woman of Proverbs, or just a package of dental floss.

Suggested Reading List

Coughran, JoAnne. *Victory at the Supermarket.* Wheaton, Ill.: Tyndale House Publishers, Inc., 1983.

Ellis, Iris. *Save on Shopping Directory.* Aurora, Ill.: Caroline House, 1970.

Felton, Sandra. *The Messies Manual: The Procrastinator's Guide to Good Housekeeping.* Old Tappan, N.J.: Fleming H. Revell, 1984.

Fooshee, George and Marjean. *You Can Beat the Money Squeeze.* Old Tappan, N.J.: Fleming H. Revell, 1980.

Jones, Pam, and Young, Peggy. *Sidetracked Home Executives.* New York: Warner Books, Inc., 1977.

MacGregor, Malcolm. *Training Your Children to Handle Money.* Minneapolis: Bethany House, 1980.

MacGregor, Malcolm, and Baldwin, Stanley C. *Your Money Matters.* Minneapolis: Bethany House, 1977.

Proulx, Annie. *What'll You Take for It?* Charlotte, Vermont: Garden Way Publishing Co., 1981.

Rushford, Patricia H. *The Care & Feeding of Sick Kids.* Palm Springs, Calif.: Ronald N. Haynes, Publishers, Inc., 1983.

VanCaspel, Venita. *The Power of Money Dynamics.* Reston, Va.: Reston Publishing Co., Inc., 1983.

Wallace, Joanne. *Dress With Style.* Old Tappan, N.J.: Fleming H. Revell, 1983.

The National Supermarket Shopper